Andy Goram

Andy Goram

"Scotland's For Me"

as told to
Simon Pia

SPORTSPRINT PUBLISHING
EDINBURGH

Acknowledgements

Our thanks to Scotsman Publications Limited for assistance with illustrations in this book.

ISBN 0 85976 315 3

Phototypeset by Beecee Typesetting Services
Printed in Great Britain by Bell & Bain Ltd., Glasgow

Contents

CHAPTER ONE

Bypass a l'Italia

Six words said it all. 'Jim's playing because of his experience.' It hit me like a thunderbolt. As I sat there stunned I didn't hear another word Andy Roxburgh said. We were sitting in a suite at the Hotel Bristol in Rapallo. Jim Leighton, Bryan Gunn and myself had trekked up to the manager's suite to hear what the team would be for Scotland's first game in the 1990 World Cup.

All the months of preparation were behind us now. The success of the early qualifying games and then the series of setbacks that had struck in Zagreb, Paris and against Egypt were history now.

What every player dreams of lay ahead, the chance to play in the game's greatest tournament. Billions of people around the world would be glued to their televisions for the next month as the greatest show on earth got on the road. Some of the world's greatest footballers have missed out on a World Cup appearance, so all professionals appreciate what a great honour it is to be there.

What hurt most of all was that I had come so close. Deep down I knew all along this would probably happen, but I had still hoped it might turn out differently. So many other people in football and the press thought so as well.

My mate Jim Leighton had distinguished himself as Scotland's goalkeeper for years. His performance in Mexico in 1986 had made a lot of the so-called English pundits eat their words when it came to dishing out stick against Scottish goalkeepers. I had been glad to act as Jim's deputy. We had roomed together for five years

1

with the Scotland party and you soon get to know somebody really well in these circumstances. I respected Jim and had learned a lot from him.

However, in the last season Jim's form had become a major issue. As Manchester United struggled to re-establish themselves as a force in English football, Jim was on the receiving end of a lot of criticism. His performances in the Scotland team had been questioned as well, and then there was the bombshell when he was dropped by Alex Ferguson for the replay of the English cup final.

I was torn down the middle. I had played well all season with Hibs and felt my form had been improving all the time. Whenever I had got a chance to play for Scotland I felt I more than held my own. So far I had never let my country down. The reason I had originally moved to Hibs from Oldham was to improve my prospects with Scotland so I could be on Andy Roxburgh's doorstep banging on the door to get into the team. The move had cost me my marriage. It was selfish of me as I had put my career first. Sometimes I look back and wonder if I made a mistake. Anyway I had invested so much in realising my dream, I thought I deserved a place, but then again if I didn't, who else would?

Then again no one likes to see a friend take the abuse that Jim Leighton had to put up with. He was under tremendous pressure and got slaughtered in the press. I felt a lot for Jim yet at the same time was desperate to take his place. The only thing was, I didn't want to do it this way. Yet there is no room for sentiment in football and I would be more than ready to take over the Scotland slot. Top professionals have to be very single-minded. That is understood between us and Jim would feel the same if it was the other way round.

As we left the room in Rapallo Jim stuck out his hand and said 'Sorry, mate.' He could appreciate how I felt. But Andy Roxburgh had stuck by Jim. He is renowned for his loyalty and it must have boosted Jim's confidence, which is exactly what he needed.

I was in a daze for sometime and later tried to cheer myself up by phoning my wife and speaking to my son Daniel. I also gave the lads at the Calderwood, my local in Bonnyrigg, a bell. From now on I had to pull myself together and get over the disappointment.

A World Cup training session at Rapallo — well, I had to keep in trim just in case.

I had a job to do helping Jim Leighton prepare for the Costa Rica game. I knew my chance would come and I would make sure I would take it. I've been with the squad at the last two World Cups and intend to be in America in 1994. Only this time I won't be on the bench.

CHAPTER TWO

My Father's Son

I suppose it was always odds on that if I became a footballer I would be a goalkeeper. You could say it was in my blood as my father was a goalkeeper, and it is one of life's strange coincidences that I should end up playing for Hibs, his first club. It never occured to me growing up as a Lancashire lad that I would return to the place where my father started his career. I was always aware he played for Hibs, but even when I started as a professional it never entered my head I would play for Hibs. However, when Hibs did sign me and I phoned up my father to tell him a Scottish club had put in a bid, he cut in on me saying, 'Don't tell me. It's Hibs, isn't it?' I'm not saying he was psychic, but then again it was just one of these things.

My father Lewis was actually born in Albion Road about a hundred yards from the Hibs ground and went to Norton Park School that backs right on to the main stand at Easter Road. It was while he was doing National Service after the war that he was spotted by Hibs and played for them for a while, but he never really broke through. Hibs had an abundance of good keepers at that time — Jimmy Kerr, George Farm, and, of course, Tommy Younger.

My father was loaned out to Third Lanark and went on to play a blinder in a crucial game against Hibs at Easter Road. This was season 1949/50 and Hibs were chasing for the title. They had only lost once so far and that was to Hearts in the Ne'er Day derby. As is so often the case, my dad turned it on against his old club and defied Hibs as they slumped to their second defeat of the season. Hibs never lost another game, but it proved costly as they lost the league by a point to Rangers. Anyway my Dad's display had impressed a few people and Bury bought him for £8,000.

He stayed with Bury till 1957, but his career was hampered by injury; he broke his leg twice and on one occasion it was Jimmy Hill who did the damage when they played Fulham. I know most Scots have strong opinions about Jimmy Hill, but my father's were stronger than most and he could be quite colourful, to say the least, whenever Jimmy appeared on television.

I also remember a story he told me about that time which pointed out to me that there isn't a lot of sentiment in football. When he came back to Bury's ground for the next game after he broke his leg they wouldn't let him in. He had to pay at the turnstile like any other punter.

What finished his career was his achilles tendon. He had had a lot of trouble with it and one game when Bury scored he leaped in the air to celebrate and it snapped when he landed. He was taken into Bury General and unfortunately was landed with a surgeon who had a reputation as being not too clever. He diagnosed it as a torn calf muscle. That was effectively the end of my dad's career as a professional although he went on loan to Buxton, a local amateur side. I think he conned his way in there as he was virtually playing on one leg.

He was always a real enthusiast for the game and it was a great pleasure to meet some of his old pals when I came to Edinburgh and to hear stories about him in his early days. He was a real character and very well known in Bury. In fact I grew up being known as Lew Goram's son wherever I went. He was always smiling and I was the only one who ever saw him not smiling. He was a great father and never hit me as a kid although I could be a daft 'un at times.

I like to think I take after him in certain ways, at least as a goalkeeper. Keepers do tend to be a bit different. Some would go as far as to say brainless, but I prefer to look on us as individualists, not your run-of-the-mill characters. Although football is a team game, goalkeepers tend to stick out. My father was also a bit on the short side for a keeper which I suppose is hereditary. When I first started professionally I was about 5ft 9in to 5ft 10in, but since then I have sprouted up to all of 5ft 11in. A lot of people still consider this a bit short for a keeper, but I have never felt it has held me back.

My father stayed on in Bury after he stopped playing as he had met my mother May and I was born there on 13 April 1964. Not a Friday, I hasten to add. As a kid I took to sport naturally and at about 10 or 11 started playing football for Marauders, a Bury boys' club similar to Edina Hibs. I played in goal for them, partly, I suppose, because I wanted to be a keeper like my dad. I also played outfield for another team, Radcliffe Borough Juniors. I was a friend of Danny Carr's son, the man who ran the Marauders. He went on to win half a million on the pools and the family took me as a friend of their son's on a holiday to Spain.

Although I played outfield with Radcliffe, I often went in goal if they were struggling at the back. I played centre forward and enjoyed it. I was a direct, no-nonsense centre with an up and at them attitude. To this day I still like to play outfield at training, but am well aware of my limitations. I have a theory that goalies are frustrated centre forwards. The converse of this is you also find a lot of centre forwards want to play in goal. At Hibs both Keith Houchen and Paul Kane, who had his spell up front, like to get between the sticks at training. They like to try and save rather than score and we goalies are the same.

It was around the age of 14 that I began to think I might have some future in football when I was selected for Greater Manchester Schools. My father never pushed me, but was always there if I ever wanted to ask him something. He wanted things to take their natural course and I think he always had confidence I would make it. He would regularly point things out to me about goalkeepers whenever we watched football together.

It was two teachers at Tottington School, Gordon Childs and a Mr Baxter, who helped me realise I had potential. I had a good relationship with teachers at school and really enjoyed it. Of course I got on especially well with sports teachers. I was now playing with a local team, Walton, in the Bolton Boys' Federation league as a centre forward. We won the odd cup, but were not the best team locally. When I was 15 I started playing in goal for

Like father like son — Paul Kane and I with our fathers, both former Hibs players.

Radcliffe Old Boys, a pub team, whose manager also ran the county team I got selected for. But the best part of the experience was I was a boy playing with men. I got whacked every week, but it toughened me up. I also got a lot of attention because we weren't the greatest of teams and as goalie I had plenty to do.

At this time I also started playing cricket with men in the first team for East Lancashire Paper Mill in the Saddleworth League. I think both these experiences were good for me and helped me to develop characterwise.

In my last year at school my breakthrough came. I was spotted by West Bromwich scout John Shore, who is dead now, and invited for a two-week trial and signed a schoolboy form.

The hardest part for me when I joined West Brom was leaving my home town, Bury. Everyone knew my dad there and when I walked through the streets I would overhear people referring to me as Lew Goram's lad. I was never referred to as me. Later on when I had signed for both West Brom and Lancashire cricket club my dad came home one day and complained someone had referred to him as Andy Goram's dad. That was my dad giving me a boost but I realised I now had my own identity.

As a young lad I had wanted to play for Leeds but that was because they were the top team at that time. The team I supported after Bury was Manchester United. However, becoming a professional footballer was a big enough thrill. When I went to West Brom my idol was Bryan Robson just like all the other young lads. He was the man who made things tick and he was to show over the next decade what a great player he was. His brother Gary played in the youth team with me. I also thought the keeper there at that time, Tony Godden, was different class and, of course, there was Atko. Ron Atkinson had made a name for himself as a flamboyant manager. I was in awe of him as a kid and even now he has that something about him when he walks into a room. He is just one of those people in football who have that special quality. Call it charisma or whatever you like.

I was naturally very excited at what lay ahead, but the hardest part as a young kid was leaving my mum and dad for the first time. When I went down to the Midlands I didn't know anyone and went into digs with another keeper, David Carlisle. I found the pre-season training a bit different from what I was used to but enjoyed it. I couldn't believe it when we had to clean out dressing rooms and the boots every day after training. I looked on it as cheap labour. I might as well have been a skivvy. All I wanted was to play in goal but here I was cleaning and mopping up all the time. It was definitely the worst part of being an apprentice. Needless to say I was the worst at it and it was a reputation that was to stick with me.

Atko had moulded West Brom into one of the most attractive teams in England at the time with class players like Tony Godden, Brendan Batson, John Wyle, Ally Robertson, Derek Steatham, Remi Moses, Bryan Robson, Ally Brown, Tony Brown, Laurie Cunningham, Cyril Regis, Peter Barnes and Gary Owen. As an apprentice I had little direct contact with Atko. My first chance came with a close-season trip to Kuwait. I was taken as reserve for Tony Godden as the usual reserve keeper was involved in some other important game. I was made to feel at home and Gary Owen and Peter Barnes looked after me. That year we got to the semi-final of the F.A. Youth Cup but were beaten by Aston Villa. On the plus side we won a tournament in Germany.

At that time there were 30 apprentices at the club and in the long run there was a huge failure rate. I think if you can get through your first year in football you are half way there. It may be difficult to settle in but I learned in my first year football is a job. Before it had purely been for my enjoyment, but now it was my career. Three people at West Brom looked after the apprentices — Roy Horobin, the youth development officer, Albert McPherson, a great old Scotsman, and Ken Hodgkinson. Albert was a typical winner who sorted us out on the training pitch and Horobin looked after us off the pitch.

That was the season West Brom reached the semi-final of the cup and lost out to Arsenal. That was not the only blow for West Brom as Atko moved on to Manchester United only to take with him Bryan Robson and then Remi Moses.

I was about to learn one of football's basic lessons. Players are continually moved on and off the club and international stage as if they were on a conveyor belt. In due course West Brom appointed Ronnie Allen and he released me. To say I was gutted would be an understatement and I headed back to Bury. I was hurt by what had happened, but did not feel that I was a failure and felt sure I would make it elsewhere.

Before I had joined West Brom Colin MacDonald, Oldham's chief scout and a former Burnley and England keeper, had watched me. He couldn't make up his mind about me before I went to West Brom, but he told me when I signed if anything happened and things did not go quite right I should get in touch with him. Meanwhile Bury had contacted my father when they heard I was free so I went down to see their manager Jim Iley and his assistant Wilf McGuiness. When I got there Wilf told me the manager would just be along in a minute. He kept me waiting for over an hour and still hadn't turned up. Supposedly he was playing snooker so I just got up and went home. Basically I didn't like the attitude there. I never spoke to the manager, but if I had I could well have followed in my father's footsteps. Although I had missed out then, little did I know the chance to do so would come my way again.

It was then that my father contacted Colin MacDonald. Oldham were the longest-serving second division side at the time and I was delighted to get another chance especially as I was signing as a professional. I thought I would not have to do the apprentices' jobs now, but I had to, which proved a real sickener. However, a great spell lay ahead of me with Oldham. I was to learn so much and meet some great people at a club which must have one of the best atmospheres going.

It's not all fun being a professional footballer.

CHAPTER THREE

Team from a Town of Chimneys

Jimmy Frizzel, a local legend, was still manager in my first season at Oldham. He was Oldham as far as a lot of people were concerned and he had been with the club in some form or another for 22 years.

Jimmy was the hard man and Bill Taylor, his assistant, had the softer approach. They were a good double act. Bill was well respected and has since died from a brain tumour. Jimmy Frizzel used to regularly have a go at me. He said I had my braces tied to the back of the net. As far as Jimmy was concerned I would be coming for a cross, then I would go back, then forwards again as though I was on a piece of elastic.

But when you're young you can afford to make a lot of mistakes. At that age you can't do anything wrong. Your mistakes are put down to your youth and if you do well it gets exaggerated. My first season was the easiest and I played in our three final games. My first-team debut came against Charlton at home. I was nervous as a kitten but I was lucky my father helped calm me down and I appreciated having somebody to talk to who understood what I was going through. Like any other young player I hardly slept at all the night before. The closer I got the worse it became. Jimmy Frizzel was different class in the way he handled me and we drew 0-0. The next two games were not as bad and we ended the season in mid-table. Having had a taste of first-team football I was raring to go in the new season. There was a great shock, though, awaiting us. Jimmy Frizzel had left as manager. I don't know what happened but maybe the board felt they needed a change. Not many people at Oldham know the reason behind it.

I will always remember Jimmy Frizzel as the man who took a chance and gave me my league debut. He was a brilliant character. He would come round the players bawling and screaming at everyone. Then Bill Taylor (somebody I wish I could have known better) followed him round and calmed them down with a joke. It was probably the ideal partnership. Jimmy had run Oldham for years on a shoestring and will always be one of the great names of Oldham Athletic.

Once again I felt I would have to prove myself to a new manager. It's something all players are apprehensive about. Some managers like you, others don't. It is as simple as that. There were some players at Oldham who thought they were there for life. Frizz had liked the way they played, so they thought they would be okay. However, every manager brings his own ideas and if you do not show you are receptive to them you will usually find your UB40 waiting for you at the door.

Going into the pre-season Joe Royle, the new manager, told me he would be getting another keeper as he wanted more experience. It was a let down as I thought I would be in. Peter McDonnell, the previous season's keeper, had moved on and Joe brought in on loan Martin Hodge from Everton.

Although I was only with Martin Hodge a short time, he taught me a lot. He made me realise what being a professional really meant. Martin was not the most natural of keepers, but he showed how with hard work you could do well and was the first one to impress on me the importance of grafting away at your game. Working with him did me a lot of good and I was sorry to see him return to Everton when he contracted a chest infection, although it gave me the opportunity to reclaim my first-team place.

Joe Royle told me he would still be looking for another keeper but I would be filling in for the meantime. I felt I had a month or two to prove I could do the job and convince Joe that I could handle it. After two months I had performed well, but Joe still felt I was too young. I had seemed to establish myself but there was always the chance he would bring in someone else. One thing for sure is it kept me on my toes.

I was a useless apprentice but I have always loved training.

Over the next four years life was hard at Oldham. It was always a bit of a struggle, and every year Joe had to sell players to make ends meet. I could understand why Joe was looking for a new keeper, but I was determined to show I could play and was the man for the job.

I was also fortunate to get a good press. As I've said already, a young keeper has a lot going for him. Mistakes are put down to inexperience and they exaggerate how good you are. As I began to make more of a name for myself everybody used to comment on my height. The most regular comment was 'Good keeper, but too small.' I was still only 5ft 9in. In my first away game it was really brought home to me. We were at Chelsea and their centre half

Mickey Droy came up for a corner. He was a monster of a man and stood right in front of me. I just came up to the top of the number five on his jersey. That's all I could see in front of me. I thought back to my days as an amateur, asking myself, 'Have I done the right thing?' It was a frightening experience and something all young players have to go through. I got my fair share of the usual treatment dished out to young keepers. Soon after Chelsea we played Crystal Palace and Dave Swindlehurst clobbered me in the first few minutes. Obviously the manager had told them to go out and unsettle the young lad. I was going for a cross on the six-yard line in the early stages when I caught a glimpse of Swindlehurst coming in. Next thing I knew I was coming to on the track behind the goal. I had nearly landed in the crowd. This time, though, I was looking up into faces of fans leaning over the barrier, thinking, 'This football lark was a bad decision. I should have stuck to cricket.'

But one thing I realised very quickly was how privileged I was to be under a manager like Joe Royle. Alan Ball had been quoted in the press as saying Joe was too nice to be a manager. You will certainly be hard pushed to find anyone in football who has a bad word to say about him, yet at the same time Joe has proved Alan Ball wrong. But what Ballie did say is true — you cannot meet a more likeable man in the game than him. He's a great guy both on and off the pitch. When he came to Oldham he hadn't long finished playing himself and knew how today's footballers thought and felt about the game. Also these were the years when we were struggling and that sort of pressure can twist a lot of people, but I can honestly say Joe made it a pleasure to play for him. You can imagine what a great atmosphere there must be at Oldham now that they're doing well.

Of course he did give me stick at times and we had our battles. I had a bit of a weight problem and Joe would absolutely slaughter me about it. He was relentless in his campaign to slim me down. I did hate him for a while because he kept getting on to me and there was a spell when I wanted away as I felt unhappy at the club. I didn't like it at all. I didn't really hate Joe Royle as a person, but felt I was getting victimised. I lost my form a bit and wasn't playing as well as I could do. Joe fined me and put me on a diet along with full back John Ryan who shared my fight against the flab. However, the more weight I lost the more I began to sharpen up and regain form. I hit my peak again and got down to my best weight of 12st 11lb and realised pretty soon that Joe had had my best interests at heart all along. Obviously if he hadn't rated me he wouldn't have bothered. He would have just sent me on my way as soon as possible. Overall I would say Joe's knowledge and judgement of players is excellent. He has bought players like Mark Ward for £10,000 and sold them for a quarter of a million. He knows how to motivate players — when to give someone a bollocking and when to go softly, softly. But when he used to shout and bawl I never considered it the real him. There was just something not right about it. But he knew exactly how to treat players. Everyone enjoyed working for him and had a lot of respect for him.

Billy Urmson was the assistant manager who looked after the apprentices when I joined and stayed on when Joe took over from Jimmy Frizzel. Bill is unknown to most people outside Oldham and he made a tremendous contribution to not only my own career but all the young players who have passed through the ranks at Oldham. This small, slightly balding chap with a thick Lancashire accent you could cut with a black pudding described me as the worst apprentice to pass through his grip. I'd probably agree as I have never claimed to be the most gifted guy with a mop and a bucket.

Bill used to have a right go at me both on and off the pitch and promptly knocked the chip off my shoulder within my first six months at Oldham. It was not till a few years later I realised it was for my own good. I used to complain to him that he was always picking on me, but I'll never forget his reply one time — 'The day I stop shouting at you is the day I don't care' — and I am pleased to say he never did stop shouting at me. Of all of them who helped me he was the one who got me through my time at Oldham more than anybody and affected my attitude off the pitch.

Every manager likes to have his own men and Big Joe brought in Willie Donachie who is still his assistant at Oldham. Willie immediately taught us all a lesson about what it was like to be a true professional. He was the fittest guy at the club and he was in

A wee bit posing now and again . . . .

his 30s at the time. There is nothing worse than having a trainer who can do everything you can do and at that do it better. He was another one some people would say was too nice a guy, but like Joe he knew exactly what he wanted and had a very single-minded approach. Willie taught me to train hard, be honest with myself and others and to hold my hand up when I was at fault. Too many players want to pass the buck when things go wrong and not face up to whatever is wrong with their own game and how they can improve it.

Willie had a great first touch and was a superb passer of the ball which was everything you need to know on plastic. Willie continually drove these points home to us when the artificial surface was first laid at Boundary Park, and all his efforts and persistence have now paid dividends as last season showed. Willie, and Martin Buchan to a lesser extent, taught me the importance of having the right attitude towards the game and made me realise just what can be done if you look after yourself. Both were winners and a shining example in any team.

. . . . never did anyone any harm.

With people like that at the club it would have been difficult not to settle in and enjoy my football. Oldham was a great little club with the bonus of being near my home town Bury. You could describe it as Coronation Street country and a book that came out about the club, *Team from a Town of Chimneys*, just about sums it up.

Everyone at the club, directors included, mucked in together and we would all congregate after a game at the White Hart pub just up from Boundary Park. The pub would lay on sandwiches and we would have a great crack. There was no division between the board, management, players and groundstaff. The atmosphere was like one big happy family and it is something I have missed since I came to Hibs. Joe Royle typified the family spirit, and while I know Oldham are unique in being such a close club, it hasn't deprived them of success. I do not see the need for all the hierarchies they have in football. Everyone should operate on a level pegging, each doing their own different job to the best of their abilities and realising we are all in it together.

I was also very lucky to come across Alan Hodgkinson at Oldham, the man who has had the most influence on my career technically. Joe Royle brought him to do specialist goalkeeping training and he changed my whole attitude to it. I would never have got on so well in the game without Alan. He started telling me things that were foreign to me and kept stressing the basics of good goalkeeping: how to switch your hands going for a ball and to catch it as much as possible. He was forever going on about 'corner pressure' — the pressure that you put yourself under if you don't catch the ball. Another maxim of Alan's was to go for everything as too many keepers can end up as ball watchers. He was always coming out with a little quip: 'What is life without a care, we have no time to stand and stare.'

Overall he improved my general technique. You can have all the ability in the world but bad technique will let you down. Now I reckon that if you're an average keeper but you have very good technique you can get still get on.

Another point Alan enforced was to stand up as long as possible when a player is coming through on you. This will put the pressure on them. Invariably you're forcing them into making the first move and they make a mistake. And that's what goalkeeping is all about — making as few mistakes as possible. Saving is the easy part, but what you're paid for is consistency and making no slip-ups.

During the early years with Oldham, Andy Farton was another keeper on the staff. I would say he was better than me when I was his age. But he used to moan at me all the time that he was sick of never getting a game while I was there. I told him to be patient because if anything happened to me or I was transferred he would walk into the team. When I went to Hibs, Andy took over but unfortunately got in with the wrong crowd and blew it all. It sickened me as he could have gone all the way and I know Joe Royle tried everything he could to keep him on the straight and narrow. Just before things really went wrong for him he said in the press that I taught him everything he knew. I was flattered, but a few days later I wasn't so sure about his compliment when he ended up in court on a few charges. I took quite a bit of stick in the dressing room over it, but it was nice to think I'd helped him with his game at least.

They were a great bunch of lads at Oldham and I have particularly fond memories of my old card school. Mickey Quinn, Mark Ward, Darren McDonough and I used to settle down to a few hands on the coach to away games. Mark Ward, I must put on record, is the worst card player in the world. The four of us always knew that we would eventually be sold as we were all doing well and a club like Oldham could not really afford to hold on to talented players for that long. So we agreed we would stick our transfer money in together and buy a horse. Within a year the three of them had been sold, leaving me still at the club. I was the one who held us up on our road to riches, and by the time I was transferred to Hibs, things had just moved on.

The close feeling among the lads at the club paid off on the pitch. The closer you are, I believe, the more you will actually play for each other.

A great example to all us young daft 'uns was Martin Buchan who came to finish his career at Oldham. Like Willie Donachie, Martin was an immaculate professional. I have heard people say Martin was a loner, but he never showed any evidence of it at Oldham. He was game for a laugh and used to whip out the guitar at socials. He is also the only player I know who when he played his last game threw a big do for all the lads. He paid for all the drinks and a slap-up meal, disproving to us Lancashire lads once and for all that Scots are tight.

Martin knew how to give it and take it and taught me a lesson one day. We had had a run in at training and, as boys will be boys, we had a kick at each other and a little roll around on the deck. Afterwards while he was away getting a rub down I thought I'd really sort him out and smeared linament all over his underpants. This stuff was so sore it would sting even the roughest part of your body. Lo and behold, Martin strolls out of the treatment room, but instead of changing just picks up his clothes and heads straight off to the Cliff, Manchester United's training ground, for a sauna. Seemingly he arrived there, had his sauna, got dressed and went upstairs to have a glass of milk in the bar. Just as he was raising his glass the linament started coming on. As he made a swift exit to the toilets it didn't take him long to figure out what had happened.

Sure enough he got his revenge the next day. I had just bought a brand-new pair of shoes and had been telling the lads I thought they were the best pair I'd ever had. While I was out training Martin got some six inch nails and hammered my shoes into the floor. When I was back in getting changed I started pulling my shoes on. Needless to say I knackered them completely. I turned round and there was Martin and the rest of the lads doubled over. That was us quits and, of course, it never affected our relationship. If anything we got on even better after that.

I must say Martin was one of the best readers of the game I have ever seen and I would have loved to have played behind him in his heyday. Playing alongside Martin at Oldham was Gary Hoolicken, one of the club stalwarts, a bit like Gordon Rae at Hibs. Gary had flaming red hair and was a really evil-looking character. I always thought he looked like a Tasmanian devil. Good players like Mark Ward, Dennis Irwin and Andy Ritchie had all joined the club and I could see Oldham had potential. Another player I rated was my room-mate Roger Palmer. One season he scored 17 goals from midfield and I have always been surprised a bigger club never picked him up.

When I first started playing with Andy Ritchie he still had hair. He always said if he did go bald he'd shave his head like a skinhead. I always rated him as a striker which he proved so well in Oldham's recent cup runs. Mickey Quinn was another really good striker and some lad as well. He is the sort who will score goals for anybody as he has proved at Portsmouth and Newcastle.

Buchan, though, was the top man. He was immaculate in his appearance and would have a shave every day after training. Everyone looked up to him and respected what he had to say. On one occasion John Bordin, who struggled a bit with catarrh, spat in the changing room. Martin pulled him up immediately, asking him if he would do that at home. John laughed at first, not thinking Martin was being serious, but he soon got the message the way Martin looked at him. Every footballer spits, but you would never see Martin Buchan do it. You also never saw John Bordin or any of the rest of us do it ever again in the dressing room.

Not only was there a great rapport within the club, but there was a special relationship with fans at Oldham. We'd get average crowds of 7-8,000 and about 12,000 for big games. I always got on great with them, but there was one guy who sticks in my mind. He used to stand behind the goal and slag me week in, week out. I couldn't do anything right as far as he was concerned and, no matter what, I could always hear this one voice at every home game. I used to try and catch sight of him, but I never once saw who he was. One game against Fulham in the cup I saved a penalty, tipping it by. My first thought was at least I've done something that he can't slag me for. Surely he'll let up now. Then as everyone settled down, out he came clear as a bell: 'You should have f*****g caught that one, Goram.'

I mean, what chance have you got? Some people are never satisfied and to this day I've never found out who he is. It's funny how keepers are particularly aware of the crowd because you're always fairly static. As we're in the one spot all the game we're a sitting target for any abuse and you hear a lot more than anyone else on the pitch.

There's even a group of three or four at Hibs who only seem to come along to give me a good slagging. They stand at the top left corner of the ground behind the goals at the bottom of the slope. I have always thought I have done well for the club and the fans are happy with me, but these lads, by the sound of them, couldn't get rid of me fast enough. I laugh about it when I think about it afterwards, but at times you've got to shake your head and admit there is no pleasing some fans.

Another good aspect about Oldham was I never got any hassle off the park. You could go out for a drink and no one would bother you. There was a local joke that none of the town lasses would even admit to getting off with an Oldham player. The rugby league club were far more prominent than us at that time although I'm sure things have changed in the last season or so.

The easy-going small-town life of Oldham is another thing I have missed since I moved away.

One of Oldham's claims to fame is that the ground, Boundary Park, is the highest in Britain, situated right at the foot of the Pennines. The wind there could be quite frightening and many a time I would just kick the ball out for a throw-in. If I tried to put it up the park it would just blow right back at me. One time I almost got caught out by the wind when Jim Barron, Crystal Palace's keeper, thumped a kick-out the length of the park. After that I started to have a go myself and came close on a few occasions, but I never fulfilled that particular ambition until I came to Hibs. Generally with Oldham I would kick out to the right wing unless I was having a go at goal. I consider myself good at throw-outs and it is something I work on.

As well as being so high up it always seemed to be raining and there was a permanent cloud hanging overhead. I was delighted when they put down the artificial surface as the ball ran a lot truer, the bounce was better and it suited ball players. But I didn't like training on it and often players would pick up a really nasty burn. It definitely gave Oldham a home advantage, but I felt teams came with the wrong idea and adopted a negative attitude. Whenever they got beaten they would say the pitch is a joke which I always reckon is an easy get out. We would work on simple things like a good first touch, and as passes run truer on a plastic pitch, we concentrated on long passing sessions at training.

Also at Oldham we played the same system week in, week out. If the system went wrong we would get beaten, it was as simple as that. If we played it well, we would win. When I came up to Scotland I found it very different with Hibs changing their system of play from one week to the next. It's hard enough playing and sticking to one system without having to change weekly. For a goalie it can be confusing because some weeks you'll play with only three at the back and five in midfield. Other weeks it's four at the back and the next one it might be five with only one man up front.

The big game at Oldham was with Manchester City who were in the second division at the time. It was the nearest we came to a derby, but when I moved to Edinburgh the Hibs v Hearts game proved to be bigger in every way. Leeds United was the other big one and for these two games we would get 20,000. Some of the grounds we visited in the second division were in a shocking state, but you got the big-time atmosphere when you went to Hillsborough, St James Park or some of the London clubs. However, a reminder of how we were a small club was I never went on tour with Oldham whereas it's an automatic part of life for Premier League clubs.

But despite that it didn't mean you didn't get a chance to play against the best. In the pre-season 1984-85 we beat Liverpool 1-0 in a friendly and thought we were it. Any notion of us being 'Jack the lads' was soon dispelled when we were drawn against them in the Milk Cup and received the biggest lesson in football any of us had ever had. They beat us 3-0 at Anfield and we hardly touched the ball in the first half-hour. Then they came and promptly cuffed us 5-2 at Boundary Park. Although I know Kenny Dalglish hates artificial surfaces, I never heard him moaning after that one.

My most memorable game with Oldham was the second leg of the play-offs in the first year they were introduced. We had been in the top three all season and would have been promoted under the old system, but here we were facing Leeds in the semi-finals of the play-offs. I have especially clear memories of both those games as a goalkeeper because I was up against one of those players that had the old 'Indian sign' over me. Ask any goalie and they will tell you there are some guys who just always seem to score against them. With me it was Keith Edwards, and sure enough in the last second of the first leg at Elland Road he pops one in to give Leeds a 1-0 win.

In the replay we went 2-0 up with a minute to go. But then they kicked off, knocked the ball wide and sent a cross over. Somebody nodded down, and, who should be there but Keith Edwards to volley it in?

The Oldham fans and some of the players were still celebrating when the ball went in, but that goal meant Leeds went through on away goals. It was a sickening end to what had been one of the best nights ever at Boundary Park. The place was heaving with fans hanging from the floodlights as we anticipated our best chance of success so far. I was actually up, standing on the fence behind the goal celebrating with the fans when the second went in and had to get down sharpish for the kick-off.

There was total depression in the dressing room afterwards and I got the most drunk I have ever been in my life that night. Keith Edwards had previously scored against me when he was with Sheffield United and he was to do the same again when we met in the Premier League when he was with Aberdeen. I had begun to hate the sight of him, and just when I thought I'd finally seen the last of him Hibs played Hull City in a pre-season friendly. Needless to say Hull got a penalty and who should take it but Keith bleeding Edwards? Everytime we play he scores against me. It's one of these things. I just can't put my finger on why it happens.

There were a few other players I didn't like playing against, but that was for other reasons. Bobby Campbell of Bradford City was one of the nicest guys you could meet off the park, but let's say he had a very meaty approach to the game. On the pitch he was a terror and he always made sure he battered me a beauty.

Big Noel Blake of Portsmouth was another one. One game I thought I'd been fouled at a corner and got up to have a go at whoever did it. I hadn't seen who it was but then I clocked Noel who's the size of a house. He just laughed as he could see I was rapidly re-evaluating the situation. I was glad he brushed it off as he could have had me for breakfast.

In my first few seasons I was naive and got knocked about a bit. Bill Urmson encouraged me to get stuck in and stamp my authority in the box so anyone coming in knew it was a battlefield. It's basic psychology. A player is less likely to come in on you, trying to catch you with a boot or an elbow if he knows you're looking out to protect yourself. After I had sorted that out I was relatively injury-free until I picked up an injury against Blackburn Rovers. Ian Mellor had broken clean through the defence, but had over-hit the ball a bit. I came for it and he started sliding in. I put my foot in front of me to stop him hitting my body, but his boot caught the underside of my foot. It dragged my foot right up and tore the ligaments in my ankle on both sides. I was out for a couple of months and made the big mistake of coming back too soon. The ligaments went again in the first game against Huddersfield and I was out for the rest of the 1984/85 season.

My knee operation at Hibs, which was a minor operation, is the first problem I have had since then. Although I didn't mind the rough and tumble on the park I can be a bit of a feartie off it. I have a phobia about needles. Once I got a knock on the collar bone and couldn't move my neck so I needed injections. I couldn't bear to look and had to take the injections lying down. It was horrendous. I would far rather face Bobby Campbell or Noel Blake any day.

I owe so much to Oldham and Alan Hodgkinson for helping me mature as a keeper. I also took notice of other keepers to see what I could pick up. Naturally I admired Ray Clemence and Peter Shilton, but I really liked Pat Jennings who used every part of his body to make a save. Another big favourite was Bruce Grobbelaar. A lot of people call him a clown, but Liverpool have won just about everything and you can't do that with a poor keeper. Bruce makes unbelievable saves and comes for crosses most keepers would never dream of going for. The reason Grobbelaar has more chance of dropping crosses is because he goes for so many.

What all these players have to get to the top of their profession is a certain attitude of mind and determination. I think it's the key factor in a professional footballer. Your success depends on 10% ability — let's face it, you must have it in the first place to be a professional. Then there is the 20% luck factor — being in the right place at the right time, being injury-free etc.

Most of all, though, 70% depends on attitude. Problems off the pitch may affect some players but I have never let it get to me. When I left Oldham I lost my marriage and my son, but I never let it affect me on the pitch. It was the same when my father died. Of course on both occasions I was gutted off the park, but I made sure it didn't affect my performance. I think I'm quite solid in that respect and on the pitch I aim to be totally single-minded. What happens off it is my own life and for me to deal with. It's nobody else's business. I just make sure I don't carry over any problems from my private life into my job as a professional footballer.

As a professional I was very happy at Oldham, but I was always wanting to move on to test myself at a higher level. I got my international breakthrough at Oldham first with England's Under 21s, then came the chance of a lifetime to play for Scotland. During my time with Oldham I won four caps — East Germany, Holland, Romania, Brazil — and was a member of the World Cup squad that went to Mexico in 1986. At the time one of my biggest fans in the media was Tommy Docherty. The Doc would lavish praise on me and very flatteringly named me as the keeper for his all-time Scottish team in a press article before the 1986 World Cup. A bit premature, perhaps, but that's the Doc for you. I used to see quite a bit of him after games at Boundary Park and he always gave me total encouragement, telling me there were no limits to how far I could go.

CHAPTER FOUR

Going Back to My Roots

There had been a lot of talk in the press that several clubs were interested in me with names such as Tottenham and Arsenal being bandied about.But there was only one real offer. That was from Everton but Joe Royle knocked it back as he did not consider £225,000 was enough.

I had broken through into the Scotland team at Oldham, but felt my career needed another push. Despite the good times with them I felt I would be limited if I stayed at Boundary Park. I had also watched other players move on while I seemed to be getting left behind and was desperate to move up a grade. I wasn't happy and my form slumped in the first nine games of the 1987/88 season.

Then in early October I came home from a reserve game one night and Joe Royle was on the phone to tell me a Scottish team had come in with a bid. At first I thought it might be Rangers because I had heard rumours that they were interested in me.

But it turned out it was Hibs and Joe told me he thought I should take it. Both clubs had already agreed the terms and we could go up to Scotland in the morning to meet them.

I was due to see my father the next day so I phoned him to tell him I couldn't make it as I was going up to Scotland. It was unbelievable as before I could say anything he said, 'You're going to Hibs, aren't you?' I asked him how he knew and he told me he just had a feeling. He wished me luck and we chatted for a while about Hibs and I knew he liked the idea of me playing for his old club.

27

I didn't know much about Hibs except what my father had told me, but I did know they were a club with a great tradition.

The next day Joe Royle and I took the train up to Glasgow and met Hibs manager Alex Miller, his assistant Peter Cormack, Jim Gray, managing director, and Cecil Graham the club secretary at the Holiday Inn in the city centre. Joe and Peter Cormack knew each other from their days together at Bristol City so they went off for a chat and left me to talk terms with the others.

I must say I was really impressed with the way they sold Hibs to me. They told me how they were going to make Hibs a great club again and I was just the first of their big signings. I felt I was not in the position to make big claims from Hibs as they were taking a chance on me. Despite my Scotland appearances I was still relatively unknown.

Hibs were also the first club to come in with an offer which tallied with the £325,000 Oldham wanted for me. I also realised the fans would probably have preferred a forward for the money Hibs were laying out.

We talked for two hours and I signed on the dotted line. Looking back on it now I feel a bit bitter about that meeting in the Holiday Inn. Hibs got me on a cheap contract, but I didn't mind that as I was really keen to play in the Premier League. It was the plans they had for the future and the promises they made me. They never fulfilled half of them and that has always disappointed me. I don't blame Alex Miller for it and have always found him to be an honest man.

Over the next two seasons we were to have the makings of a very good team at Easter Road with some class players, but there was never the necessary back-up from the board.

Everyone now knows that things had got totally out of control behind the scenes. However, I really began to lose faith in the club when they spent money from the share flotation on pubs and restaurants in the south of England rather than on new players.

At the time Hibs had also been interested in signing Ian Andrews and he had come up to see Hibs play Celtic. It was a 1-1 draw with Hibs seemingly playing Celtic off the park. However, Ian preferred at that momement to stay in England and try and forward his England career. Joe Royle then moved in and phoned

Alex Miller introduces his new signing and Hibs' biggest buy to date.

Peter Cormack to tell him they could have me for the same money and I was a different animal altogether.

When I look back on it I'm surprised Peter didn't put the phone down on Joe straight away. The only time Hibs had seen me was in the Isle of Man a year before when they beat Oldham 3-0. That day I had a stinker. Gordon Rae scored his first goal for three years, Johnny Collins nutmegged me and to top it all Mickey Weir scored with a header.

Ian Andrews was to change his mind about Scotland and joined Celtic. At the time I think a lot of people thought Ian was a better keeper than me and Celtic had got the better deal. Ian had a good reputation in England and at one stage Liverpool had been after him. Unfortunately he came to Celtic at a bad time and he will always be remembered for the one game at Ibrox when they lost 5-1. I think he was to blame for only one goal that day, but you will never be forgiven if you make mistakes in that game. He had cruel luck and I would have liked to see him get the chance to play in a good Celtic team.

On the day I signed for Hibs a tribunal agreed on a price for Mickey Weir's transfer to Luton and they used the money to pay for me. Little did I know I was making one of my biggest mistakes as I put pen to paper in the Holiday Inn. I was virtually signing away my marriage.

I phoned my wife immediately after the deal went through and she put the phone down on me. We had been going through a bad time anyway and here I was deciding what I thought was our future without discussing it with her. I realise it was selfish of me but I felt the move was the right decision for me. My wife had no intention of moving. She's very close to her family and didn't want to move away from them.

When I look back on the decision and realise it would cost me my marriage I probably wouldn't have done the same thing now. But I just dived straight in. It had all happened so quickly. My career had slipped a bit and here was a great chance opening up in front of me. The Premier League's reputation was soaring and my claim for a Scotland place would be strengthened. The die were cast and I moved up to Edinburgh a few days later.

I met the Hibs team on the Friday before they played Dunfermline. I don't think anyone had told Alan Rough that I was signing and he thought he would be playing on the Saturday. But Alex Miller called everyone together on the training pitch and said there would be one change from the team that had just beaten Motherwell 1-0 and I would be in for Roughie. I felt a bit awkward as I had got on well with Roughie in the Scotland squad and here I was coming in and pushing him out of the team. Although it's part of your job as a professional, it still is not a nice feeling. But full credit to Alan Rough as he never showed his disappointment and bore no grudge. Roughie went out of his way to help me settle in. He's an experienced pro and knows what it's all about. I think too many people forget all the points Alan Rough had saved Hibs over the years and I have been told by people who should know that he was responsible for keeping Hibs in the Premier division in his first season at Easter Road. The big man is different class and one of the funniest men I have ever met. He was a great presence in the dressing room and everybody loved him. He is one of those people that don't have to say anything to make you laugh. Just one look from Roughie and his infectious grin and you're away.

Alan Rough and I got on well together.

In my first game for Hibs I was probably more nervous than in my Scotland debut. People had told me before that Hibs were a tight team. They didn't give away many goals, but then again they didn't score many. I could hardly believe when we were 4-0 up after half an hour.I thought they had been taking the mickey out of me. That game I never had a shot to save till the last minute. I had wanted to get a few saves under my belt, but that would have to wait till the next game.

However, I was impressed by my new colleagues, not least the goal scorers Paul Kane, Eddie May, George McCluskey and John Collins.

I had just come up from Oldham, a team who had just missed out on promotion. In my first nine games of the season I hadn't played too well and I was worried that if I messed up my first game it could affect me. But it was an ideal start and, being superstitious, I knew I'd develop a new routine at Hibs.

If I win one week I'll wear the same clothes, even socks and underpants — washed of course — to the next match. I'd also wear the same strip and if we lost I would change it, even my gloves. I'd also have exactly the same pre-match meal as long as we were winning.

But there came a stage when we couldn't win a game and I went through every combination with the strip and clothes I wore to the game that I could think of. I even ended up wearing two odd gloves. In my pre-match warm-up I liked to go out early with Roughie for a so-called warm-up. If I was lucky I would get three shots from him in half an hour. But in my early games Roughie was very good at relaxing me. He would blether about what happened the night before and what was running in the 3.30 that afternoon.

I didn't need any reminding that I had stepped up a grade at Easter Road as my second game was the Edinburgh derby. I couldn't believe how no one was giving Hibs a chance as I was unaware of recent derby history. Hibs hadn't won one for ten years. Everyone was going on about Hearts and they were top of the league at the time. I was interviewed on television the night before and said I couldn't believe all the talk about Hearts. They were just another team and we would go out and beat them.

I hadn't experienced such a build-up in a club game before, but I really relished the big match atmosphere. The game was a cracker with Hibs winning 2-1. Eddie May put us in front before John Robertson equalised and then Paul Kane rose up to crash in a header from a corner. There was champagne in the dressing room afterwards, something I hadn't experienced at Oldham.

The same day there was the infamous punch-up at Ibrox between Messrs McAvennie, Butcher and Woods with Graham Roberts in a supporting role. There had been none of that down at Oldham. It was more like handbags at twenty paces. I thought, 'This is the league for me!' I like to thing I'm a battler and a winner, and if this was what was happening every week there was no way the Premier League would be boring. Another encouraging sign for me that I had made the right decision was that Andy Roxburgh, Scotland's manager, had said in the press he was glad I had moved to Scotland. He had actually spoken to me a month before I moved and I understood from the conversation that if I came up to Scotland I would have more of a chance to prove myself. I also don't think Andy Roxburgh was a great fan of plastic pitches and felt it caused more wear and tear on your joints training on it. However, I thought for a while that I

Hullo Hibbies! I greet the crowd before my debut against Dunfermline.

had missed out. I had joined Hibs to really stake my claim for the Scotland spot, and the next thing I knew I was out of the squad and missed the next three games. It actually proved a blessing in disguise because it made me realise how lucky I was to have been in the team in the first place. When I was out I missed it so much and realised how many other players would like to get my place.

But it was time to knuckle down and establish myself with Hibs. They had just signed Neil Orr from West Ham whom I knew from the English second division. I didn't really know what to expect from the others. I was struck by the skill of many players like John Collins, but it was George McCluskey who made an immediate impact. I thought he had loads of skill but by now he was getting past it. I would have liked to have played with him in his prime. 'Beastie' was also a real character in the dressing room and helped create a good atmosphere among the boys. The Glasgow lads who travelled through together tended to be a bit livelier. I knew Joe McBride from Oldham whom we called 'the hurdler' as he wasn't the bravest of players, but he was another with loads of skill. Joe was a chirpy wee guy, a typical winger who was great at crossing and dead ball situations. Another one from the wild west is Graeme Mitchell. A quiet lad at first sight, but a real pest when you're out for drink with him. The Hibs lads were a great bunch, but they didn't mix much, unlike the Oldham lads.

I was soon brought down to earth after a heady start with Hibs and was glad it happened away from home. We lost to St Mirren with Ian Ferguson scoring twice. People immediately said I was a waste of money and I'm sure a lot of Hibs fans had their doubts. It gave me a real boot up the backside and I learned not to get too complacent. Things had been going a wee bit too well. I realised the Premier League was not going to be a joy ride after such a good start. Alex Miller questioned me about the goals as it was the first time I had messed up. I think he was wondering, 'What have I done here buying this mug?' However, I like to think that since then I have done the business for him. I have always got on well with him although he has taken some stick from the fans.

He is the most successful manager at Easter Road since Eddie Turnbull, so who's to say he isn't on the right track? In my second season he got us to the quarter finals of the Skol Cup, the semi-finals of the Scottish Cup and into Europe for the first time in eleven years. Yet many of the fans still wanted him sacked. It baffled me. With any other team it would have been a successful season. I couldn't believe how much some fans had it in for him; I think a lot of it is not to do with his record, but the fact that he was a Rangers player. I know fans complain about defensive

Where am I? John Brown had just knocked me out in a collision at Ibrox. Rangers scored while I was having 40 winks.

tactics, but there is a limit to what you can do with the players you've got. He hasn't exactly had money to get good players and many a time he has had to shuffle the pack because of injuries. I would rate him as very good tactically, and he looks on each game as a game of chess where he has to outwit the other manager.

When we played Hearts he dropped Mickey Weir and John Collins and the fans went daft. Yet we went and beat them but the fans forgot their original attitude. Obviously he makes mistakes, but so do others. However, he gets crucified for it. He is also not the dour character he can come across as. I have been at a few social occasions with him and he is very good company. He's conscious though of keeping a distance, which is understandable.

Soon after my arrival at Hibs I had my first taste of Ibrox. We lost 1-0 with Robert Fleck nutmegging me for the game's only goal. I have loved playing at Ibrox ever since and Hibs always seem to do well against Rangers. Part of that is that Rangers let you play as they come at you. In my first meeting with Rangers I knew Graeme Souness and Davy Cooper from the Scotland squad and after the game they wished me well in settling at Hibs. The Premier League is so small that you soon get to know most players, especially if you've played with Scotland at both Under

21 and full international level. Although it's an extremely competitive league, there is a friendly atmosphere and we have a laugh at each other during games. Two in particular I have a crack with are Ally McCoist and John Robertson. Also when I came here I made an effort to get on with people.

It was around this time the squad for the Bulgaria game in the European Championship was announced. It was the first time since I had been originally picked I was not selected. I was taking it for granted I would be in. You usually find out from teletext what the squad is and the official letter arrives the next day. When I first looked at the teletext that day I immediately checked it again to see if it was right. My name was missing and it hurt a lot, but I was more determined than ever to establish consistent form with Hibs.

However, we took a bit of a dip after out good run and lost to Motherwell and Dundee. Then there followed a rather eventful visit to Aberdeen and an encounter with that man Keith Edwards again. He scored against me again, but as he came clean through he put the ball past me and I brought him down.

Alex McLeish and Willie Miller still say to this day that I just went for him, but I was too slow going for the ball and hit him. Edwards went down and all the Aberdeen players started screaming at me. Scotland's best-known referee charged the length of the pitch accompanied by Alex McLeish to try and get me sent off. I appealed to the other referee on the pitch that day — the one in black — not to do anything stupid as it would spoil the game. The referee agreed and booked me. I was booed every time I touched the ball after that.

As a goalie you have to look after yourself without going over the top. You can't go for balls expecting an easy time or you'll get battered. I'm quite a broad lad and can look after myself, but I don't go looking for trouble. There is none of your Harold Schumacher about me. Some may think keepers are over-protected, but they often get a real tanking. More often than not if you think about it the keeper is the one who ends up flat out getting treatment. I had it pumped into me at Oldham that a good keeper dominates his box and looks after himself. My father used to say we had it easy compared to the old days when they were regularly knocked into the back of the net.

The most striking thing about the Scottish game was how physical it was. The tackling was crazy and I thought players were getting away with murder. As I watched bodies flying about during my first game I was just glad to be in goal. In my first few games referees were letting tackles go while stretchers were coming out on the touchline. I soon got used to it and realised it's all part of the Scottish make-up. The fans seem to like it. They don't want to see players with handbags and lipstick and you can see them turn on a player who shies out of a tackle.

The Scottish game continued to provide plenty of drama. In my first home game against Celtic we were trailing 1-0, but were just beginning to get back into the game when I heard a bang behind me. At first I thought it was a firework. I noticed some smoke and the next thing people were piling onto the pitch. I now thought it was a fight until my eyes started streaming. We soon realised it was CS gas and the game was abandoned as people were treated on the pitch. My father was up for the game, but was right at the other side of the ground in the stand. He later claimed he was affected and had to get down to the players' lounge. He also badly needed a drink.

He had the hanky out wiping his eyes and the woman behind the bar gave him a whisky, but he kept needing another to settle himself. Of course there was nothing wrong with him, but he ended up having four or five whiskies on the house.

My father wasn't the only fly 'un that day. As I was coming off I saw one lad helping a guy with a leather jacket. The guy was saying, 'I can't see, I can't see.' The other guy suggested he take his jacket off as it would help him cool down and breathe more easily. I couldn't believe the nerve of him as he helped the blinded guy off with his jacket and then took off up the pitch. Meanwhile the blinded guy is lying on the ground not knowing what's happening.

We were very lucky that nobody was seriously hurt that day, and I thought the club and the fans handled themselves very well.

Not long after I was pleased to play in Jim Duffy's testimonial game where Andy Roxburgh was a spectator. I roomed with Jim when he played as an over-age player for the Under 21s and he is one of the nicest blokes in the game. His injury was a cruel blow and it always seems to happen to the nicest guys. Andy Watson of Hibs is another case in point. Ironically I almost picked up an injury in the testimonial game when Alan Lawrence dived in on me. He gave my ankle a bad knock and I turned on him to bawl him out for it. But he was lying there moaning 'my knee, my knee.' It was ripped open from one side to the other. I thought, 'What am I complaining about?'

Back in the league we slipped again, losing 2-0 to Rangers, and Neil Orr was sent off. I had played twelve games with him and not rated him that highly as he didn't create anything. When he was suspended I reassessed my opinion. I didn't realise what a good job he did until he was missing. He breaks up an awful lot, and although he's a defensive midfield player, he does score from time to time. Neil is also quite a cool customer. Before a night game against Rangers everyone was a bit on edge psyching themselves up. Someone was missing, then I spotted Neil out in the corridor practising his golf swing. He seemed more bothered about that than the game ahead of us.

It was also around this time there was talk of Hibs being interested in Charlie Nicholas. I asked him about it at Jim Duffy's testimonial dinner, but Charlie laughed it off. It was obvious he had something sorted out and was soon to join Aberdeen. I would have loved to see Charlie at Easter Road. The first time I had really seen him was in Mexico in 1986. Charlie was superb in training and if he hadn't got injured in the first game against Denmark I think he could have made the difference as to whether we qualified or not.

Charlie has had his critics, and maybe he isn't as quick over 10 or 15 yards as he used to be, but give him a yard or two and he can wreak havoc. I would rather play with him than against him and he has begun to develop a bit of the Keith Edwards syndrome as he nicks quite a few goals against me. Charlie has received the champagne tag in his time, as have Maurice Johnston and Frank McAvennie. Far too much is made in the press of players having a drink. Most players get to the stage where they know how drink affects them. If you're out five nights a week and you get the man of the match award, there isn't much anyone can say. Look at George Best, possibly the greatest player in Britain since the war.

Under siege from Celtic. I soon realised the Premier League was no place for the faint hearted.

It was other pressures that drove him out of the game. Now Paul Gascoigne has hit the scene as one of the most gifted players for years. Everyone knows he likes a drink, but the game in England has been crying out for a player like him. Gazza is something special and who knows what makes him tick, but obviously he is the best judge of that. Some players I know are totally unaffected by drink. My old room-mate at Oldham, Roger Palmer, likes one yet he never puts an ounce on and is a brilliant trainer.

As long as you know your own limitations and don't let it catch up with you. I'll give you an example. When I had first moved to Hibs I was put up in the Hilton, but I didn't like it at all. No one would talk to you and I wouldn't have minded an occasional conversation. Anyway I got Hibs to move me to the Lady Nairne Hotel which was totally different. I was so at home there I could have cooked my own meals in the kitchen. Anyway I used to ask them to stick a bottle of wine aside for me whenever I missed a meal as I had full board. Come the New Year I had built up quite a stock and there was a big party at the hotel. To cut a long story short I went over the score and had a few too many. It is something that has always puzzled me about Scotland. Why do you have the big derbies right at the time of the biggest booze-up of the year? Somebody is obviously trying to make footballers suffer.

The next day I played in one of the best 0-0 draws I've seen. Hearts dominated the first half and we took over in the second. It was my best game so far for Hibs and I ended up with the man of the match award. I had one bit of luck in that game when I miskicked a ball straight to John Robertson. Unusually for him against Hibs he made a hash of it. Every goalie generally makes at least one mistake in a game. Most times you're never caught out, but you never have a perfect game. One thing my father and Alan Hodgkinson drummed into me was kick every ball with the outfield players. If the ball goes to the full back follow it and play it with him in your mind. Never for a second can you afford to take your eye off the ball.

One thing that has helped my concentration is snooker. I played every day for four years at the Duck Club in Bury. I'd go in from three to six in the afternoon and come back after tea at 7.30 and stay till 11pm. Cricket is another game that helped me develop concentration. I also used to fish a lot and all anglers know you've got to keep your eye on the float. One glance away and you lose one.

The one aspect of the game where you have nothing to lose is a penalty. I can't believe it when someone misses. After all you're a professional and you have a clear shot from 12 yards. But we have all seen the world's greatest miss them. Bill Urmson at Oldham urged me to take a note of every penalty against me and where the player placed it. So I've kept a black book for this purpose ever since. It's no big secret and sometimes it goes wrong. But players are creatures of habit and if they're successful with one way of doing something they'll stick to it.

But I don't have any idea how many I've saved. I've stopped two in a row against St Mirren and then Motherwell. In the end I reckon it balances itself out and you may save half as many as you let in over your whole career. I always remember Paul Cooper of Ipswich saving eight on the run. That's some record.

The Premier League also disproved the English myth propagated by Jimmy Greaves of the duff Scottish keeper. I admired Jim Leighton already from the Scotland squad. He's a model pro from whom I've learned a lot.

Campbell Money was another I knew from international duty and he was unfortunate enough to get more than his fair share of bad luck. It was between Campbell and me who went to Mexico in 1986 and he got injured at vital times and this tipped the scales in my favour. Other keepers immediately impressed me. Pat Bonner was one. He gets annoyed at the slightest mistake he makes. Chris Woods was another and I could understand how he has felt waiting in the wings for Peter Shilton to leave the international stage. One of the younger keepers who stands out is Alan Main of Dundee United.

One keeper I really underrated at first was Theo Snelders. Alan Hodgkinson was running a coaching course at Largs for about thirty keepers and Alex Smith and Jocky Scott brought Theo along for Alan to have a look at him. Now Alan never stops going on about catching the ball. So Theo takes a spot in goal and someone fires one in straight at him about chest level. Instead of catching it Snelders punched it with both fists right back at whoever shot. Alan just shook his head while all the other keepers were looking at each other thinking, 'We have a right chance here next time we play Aberdeen if they're going to sign this guy.' For the rest of the session he didn't look at all impressive. Needless to say Theo went on to prove us all wrong and the biggest compliment you can give him is to say that Aberdeen fans soon forgot about Jim Leighton.

And of course there's Henry Smith. I feel he could have done with someone pushing him more at Hearts for his place, but Hearts have done well with him. Being a showman seems to be part of his game, but he has made some mistakes in big games. When Hearts had Nicky Walker pushing for a place, Henry went on to have one of his best seasons.

When I got my first Scottish cap Greavsie was at an Oldham game and kidded me on that now I was a Scottish keeper I would start dropping it. However, I believe we have the best set of keepers in Britain in the Premier League.

Another boost I received was when someone pointed out I was the first Hibs keeper to go four games without letting in a goal in twenty-five years. Jim McArthur had a similar shut-out in the late '70s but that was in the First Division. Goalies get the praise for a run of clean sheets but the defence deserves just as much credit and Gordon Rae, Graeme Mitchell, Gordon Hunter and Alan Sneddon certainly deserved that. Gordon Rae was to have two of his best seasons at Hibs when I first arrived and it neatly coincided with his testimonial season. Alan Sneddon is another very experienced defender. I have heard him take stick from the fans, but he showed the true mark of a pro by bouncing back to top form. He may not be the most gifted going forward but you will rarely see a winger get much out of him. Mark Walters never gets a look in against him and I have heard Davy Cooper had the same trouble.

Snoddy is one of those at the club you could put your house on. He also has some shot and can really let fly. He's a casual bloke and something that tickled me is that even his wife Allison calls him Snoddy. Her maiden name is Short and I couldn't believe it the first time I was out in company with them. She's going, 'Will you get us a drink, Snoddy?' and he's saying 'Aye, what do you want, Shortie?'

Graeme Mitchell is a cool and deceptively strong centre back. I'm sure it's his best position, but he has been pushed into midfield. No one likes playing wide on the left unless it's your natural position as you tend to get left out of the game. It's well known John Collins couldn't stand it.

When we went on to go seven games at the start of the next season Big Gaz, Mitch, Snoddy, Geebsie and I had a great time at the back. At that stage we were almost going out taking it for granted no one could get past us.

Gordon Hunter is a defender with a big future. He also happens to be the worst trainer I have ever seen, and in warm-up he's so stiff he doesn't look like an athlete at all. Everyone laughs at him but that doesn't bother Geebsie in the slightest. When it counts on the pitch, if someone puts a ball past him you can be sure Geebsie will get him. Off the park he's a very quiet lad. That is until females arrive on the scene. The Jekyll and Hyde takes over

I had always dreamed of scoring from a kick out and sure enough I achieve my ambition against Morton.

as he goes down behind a table and comes back up a different Geebsie.

Neil Cooper had initially taken over Gordon Rae's spot at the back and he was a snip at £30,000. He did a great job and is an example of how bizarre the transfer market really is.

Although Gordon Hunter has been playing more recently in the middle of the defence, I think his best position is full back. That is where his top-class recovery is useful and he can also use his pace to get forward. Young Willie Miller will do a fine job for Hibs. Everyone knew for some time he was a good player and a wee hard nut who would make it. If he turns out half as good as his namesake he should be delighted.

Not only were the goalies top-class in the Premier League. I was very impressed by many defenders. Terry Butcher doesn't need any explanation, and Craig Levein and Dave McPherson stand out. But Willie Miller and Alex McLeish are magnificent. They seem to have a telepathic relationship and are a perfect pair. Alex will go in and die for you and there is not better reader of the game than Willie Miller.

The forward pairing I had most difficulty against in my first season were Ally McCoist and Robert Fleck who never seemed to stop running. Tommy Coyne and Keith Wright were an underrated pairing. Dundee were not the best of teams but that season those two pulled them out of trouble a lot of times. Individuals such as Charlie Nicholas and John Robertson left their imprint as they regularly nicked one past me.

However, they was another striker who left his imprint for different reasons — Steve Kirk of Motherwell. For some reason we just don't hit it off on the park. The first time I played against him he came in and caught me late. So next time he came into the box I was ready and let him know who the gaffer was. From that moment on it has just grown. Some of the collisions we have had would register on the Richter scale. The lads kid me on in the dressing room before we play Motherwell that Kirk is going to sort me out. I don't need to be wound up, but that helps me get in the mood for our encounter. A lot of verbal goes on between us and I don't mind the aggro at all as long as I come out on top.

To date he has never scored against me and it's something I never stop reminding him about when we play. My best moment so far in Scottish football came when I saved a penalty off him. I laughed in his face when he missed. He was raring to take it and I couldn't have stood it if he had scored and was so pleased when I saved it. You sometimes hear people say about these situations it's nothing personal. Well, with Steve Kirk and me I can assure you it's totally personal.

I have only met him once off the park at a dinner, but we didn't really chat. I don't think either one of us wanted to.

One of the hardest shots I have ever come across happened on my first visit to Cappielow. Alex Miller warned me that Maargard shot from anywhere and he could really hit the ball. Morton got a free kick 30 yards out and I only directed two men into the wall. I soon regretted it as Maargard let loose a thunderbolt that I knew nothing about. I was lucky to stop it as it cannoned off my elbow which was numb for a week afterwards. Alex Miller had a good laugh at me afterwards as at the next free kick which was from almost the halfway line I made sure there were four men in the wall. All I can say is I wasn't taking any chances.

Cappielow and a cup tie at Dumbarton were the other side of Scottish football which balanced up the high drama I had been experiencing so far. All I can say about Boghead is it's aptly named. I've never come across a pitch like it. That was a tough one as Bertie Auld, Sons' manager at the time, wound them up and there was a bit of an edge due to Bertie's former Hibs connection. We were lucky to get away 0-0 and I was glad I didn't have to go there a couple of time a season. But we comfortably beat them 3-0 in the replay.

Hibs' new signing at that time had us wondering what he would be like due to manager Alex Miller's curious turn of phrase. Before we had played Morton he had told us to watch out for their centre who despite being a wee lad could jump like a giraffe. Have you seen a giraffe jump? Well, neither had any of the Hibs lads, but obviously the boss thought it was a saying. So when he said he had signed Gareth Evans for £80,000 we asked the boss what he was like. None of us had heard of him. The boss says 'He's really quick and can run all day and wasnae bad in the air for his size.' At this I piped in, 'Does he jump like a giraffe?' 'Aye, that's right' was the boss's reply, and he continued on as deadpan as ever. I'm still not sure if Gareth does jump like a giraffe, but he did score a header on his debut when we beat Dundee 2-1. Gareth turned out to be a terrific worker and if he could finish like Steve Archibald he would be worth a fortune as he does everything else right.

Just after Gareth's arrival our cup run came to an end when Celtic beat us 1-0 in a replay at Easter Road with Billy Stark hitting in the rebound after Peter Grant had blasted against the bar.

We had not a bad run after that, but lost against Falkirk at Brockville. By the time we met Hearts at the end of March we had lost only six goals in sixteen games. Only Celtic had a better record and they were on course to winning the double in their centenary season. The boss had signed me to tighten up the team and I felt I had made my contribution. We slipped 2-0 at home to Celtic in early April, but bounced back in our next away game which was at Ibrox. It was a game I'll remember for the wrong reasons as I was severely concussed and didn't know half of what was going on. As I went for a cross at the back post in the first half John Brown caught the back of my head, and as I collapsed onto the deck Rangers scored in an empty goal. Hibs were on the ropes because although I played on anyone could see I wasn't the full shilling. Then we lost another man as Mickey Weir got sent off for arguing. It shows what state I was in for as we came back on for the second half I asked Gordon Rae where Mickey Weir was. Big Gaz thought I was having him on at first till he realised it was genuine. His confidence in his keeper must have gone by now but we clawed our way back in and got a draw.

We then drew our next two games against Motherwell and Dundee before facing Morton in the last game of the season. This is one game I will never forget even if I live to be a hundred. The boss told us before the game we would have to score three to get our bonus. David Duff and Jim Gray carried out a public relations stunt beforehand, going round the ground waving at fans, and went in to watch the game from the terracing. A few of us were a bit cynical about it even then. Their efforts to be men of the people at one with the fans just didn't ring true. Funnily enough it almost backfired as Morton went one up. Duff and Gray must have been thinking we've made a mistake here, we could get lynched.

Then my big moment came in the 32nd minute. Neil Orr had already equalised when I thumped one up the park. It was some kick as it was up the slope. The bounce beat Dave Wylie and hit the back of the net. I couldn't believe it as I had fulfilled an ambition I had always had. Ever since I had seen Pat Jennings do it against Alex Stepney on television I had fancied it. But I felt really sorry for Dave Wylie as I wouldn't have liked it to happen to me. It nearly did once when Jim Barron of Crystal Palace hit the post from the other end.

Jim Gray swore to me after the game that just as I was about to kick, a fan had said to him I was a good buy. He'd replied, 'He's not a bad signing for £325,000 but he hasn't scored for us yet.'

There was a superb response from the crowd and every time I got the ball they were shouting for me to shoot. I was absolutely delighted to do it and I think it helped build my relationship with the Hibs fans. I had hoped the club and fans felt I was a sound keeper, but I also like to think I have a bit of flamboyance as well and can entertain.

It was the perfect end to what had been a good season for me. We finished sixth in the league on 43 points whereas the season before we were nearly relegated.

I was happy the way things were going at the club and there was a lot of optimism for next season. I had worked my way back into the Scotland squad for the Rous Cup matches against England and Colombia. Life in Edinburgh was good to me and my summer would be full as I had signed up for Penicuik Cricket Club.

A trio of Scotland goalkeepers. Jim Leighton, Bryan Gunn and yours truly.

CHAPTER FIVE

High Hopes with Hibs

If Hibs added to their pool in the coming season I was sure we would qualify for Europe. There was a real buoyancy in the camp at pre-season training although the first day back is the worst day of the year for me. The last day of the season I think, 'Oh no, it's only two months to the pre-season.' What made it even worse was that we headed off to an army camp in Dusseldorf and a rendezvous with 'Bastard Hill'. That's what we christened this 550-yard hill we had to belt up day in, day out. The first time I saw it I thought I should never have come to Hibs. I managed to pull through and Joe McBride was the only real victim, spewing up at the top. I have never been a distance runner, but keepers have to go through it like all the rest of the team.

All the running is a real drag, but you just have to get through it. Your boots give you blisters and it's usually about 90 degrees. At night I just collapse into a chair. While we were in Germany there was talk that Steve Archibald might join us. I welcomed the prospect and knew him a bit from the Mexico squad.

Some of the lads said they had heard he was a loner, but I told them they would be surprised when they met him. He's cautious with people he doesn't know but once you get to know him he's a gread lad. I felt if Hibs could get him it would be a great boost for the club and a sign that Duff and Gray were on the right track. With players of his calibre this would be the start of our success.

Anyone who looks back and doesn't think that was a good move must be off their head. Archie scored 16 goals for us in his

Showing off a new Hibs strip with Eddie May and John Collins.

first season and it was his goals that got us into Europe. Also you've got to remember he missed a lot of games through injury. The games he did play in he stood out like a sore thumb. He was head and shoulders above most of the team and that is no disrespect to the others. Archie has played at the top with Barcelona and Tottenham and every club he played at the fans loved him. He may not have been a big hit in the international team, but you could say that about a lot of players. Even Kenny Dalglish and Graeme Souness had spells when they had to take a lot of flak at international level.

Some people were sceptical as they thought he was getting on a bit, but everyone was a bit in awe when he arrived. He was a big name from Barcelona and there was something about him that said he was a top man. He was a perfectionist like Martin Buchan and his gear was always sorted out immaculately in his kit bag.

Not long after he had arrived I was driving a friend's Rolls down Minto Street in Edinburgh when this XJ6 pulled out in front of me. Driving it was a blonde guy with shades and a blonde girl sitting next to him. It was none other than Archie. The first thing he had done was get an XJ6. That sums the man up as he likes the best things in life and deserves it for what he has done. A few weeks later he arrived at training in a Rolls. The rest of us were just a little bit impressed when we compared it to our old bangers. We kidded him on that he could take us all to the training ground in it. It had been one of his ambitions to own one since he worked as an apprentice for Rolls Royce as a lad. Sure enough he had attained it and that's just the sort of guy he is.

Another occasion he was sitting out a game against Rangers, and as he had his family with him he didn't want to sit in the stand and take stick from any fans. He asked Hibs if he could use one of the new executive boxes that was lying empty down the front. Big-hearted lot that they were, Hibs refused. So Archie whips out his wallet, pays £400 on the spot for the box and invited my mother who was up for the game to join him and his family. Once again Archie proved he had a touch of class. He was big time at what was then, I am sorry to say, a small-time club.

Once the lads got to know him they realised stories about him being stand-offish were a total fallacy. He was good fun and a real wind-up expert. He and Paul Kane gave each other no end of stick and I think by the time he left they were quite close.

One thing about Archie is he is his own man. At Tottenham they had a psychologist that dealt with all the players. You had to go and see him so Archie finally does. In he walks and sits down. The psychologist leans over and says, 'Now, Steven, do tell me. How you feel at this very moment?' Archie looks him straight in the eye deadpan and says, 'Like a big brown bear.' The psychologist guy was floored. This one really had him fooled. Needless to say Archie was soon dismissed and never called back.

Being his own man, no one will tell Archie what to do. However, you will never get really close to him. Once you thought you could tell how he would react to a situation, he

Looks like I've lost it but that wee impeder John Colquhoun has fouled me.

would go and do the very opposite. He was also very private about his personal life and as far as he was concerned it was no one else's business.

At times you could see he was frustrated playing for Hibs as he would make a run, but the ball never arrived. But he was very generous with advice to players. I would ask him, as a striker, if, say, he got the ball at the near post where would he put the ball nine times out of ten. Archie would explain all the options that went through a striker's head and gave me an insight into how to handle the situation from my point of view. He was also a good dressing-room influence as a lot of the younger players were wary about speaking up if they thought something was wrong. But Archie, Gordon Rae and myself would speak up.

When the pre-season games started I returned to my old hunting grounds as we played Oldham, Bury and Walsall. I got a terrific reception from the fans on my return to Bounday Park where we won 2-1.

We had a good, steady start to the season and went seven league games without letting in a goal. Our first defeat was in the quarter final of the Skol Cup against Aberdeen in a great game at Easter Road. We played in white strips that night — Peter Cormack told us if it was good enough for Real Madrid, it was good enough for us. Charlie Nicholas scored again before Paul Kane struck a superb equaliser, and only in extra time did Grant get the Dons' winner. That night Theo Snelders made the best save I've seen in Scotland off another effort from Kano. Theo brought Kano down outside the box just like I'd done to Keith Edwards a few months earlier at Pittodrie. Kano blasted a tremendous free kick but somehow Theo turned it away. If he had tried to catch that one he would have ended up in Albion Road.

We felt aggrieved at losing to them and went up to draw 0-0 in Aberdeen the next Saturday.

After that game I was told I had won the Australian Hibs supporters' player of the year award and I thought at first 'Aye, aye I'll have to go to Australia to pick it up. That'll be a nice wee trip', but one of their lads presented it to me when he was over on holiday. I was chuffed to get it as every award is an honour.

On top of that I was selected for the Scotland squad for the first World Cup qualifier against Norway which was a vital game for us. Looking back, I think it was our most important result as it got us off on a winning run and it was two points away from home.

However, after the euphoria of the initial win in Oslo it was back to league business.

By now we had gone seven games without conceding a goal but then we lost our first league goal away to Dundee United. Raphael Meade got a penalty after colliding with Gordon Rae and myself. We thought it was an unfair decision and were a bit sick especially as our shut-out was broken in such a dubious manner. Big Gaz made amends for the penalty when he ran the length of the pitch to score the equaliser. Everyone was shouting for him to pass it because when a big centre half goes flying up the pitch like that

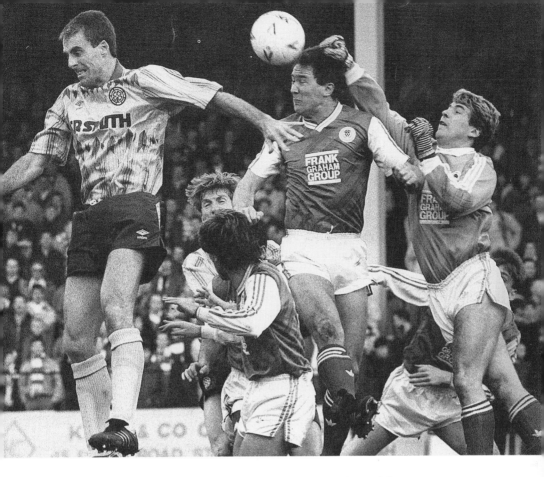

Giving Gaz a hand. With Gordon Rae in the middle of the defence we were rock solid.

you start panicking that the back door has been left wide open. I never thought he would do it, but the big man stuck away a lovely goal. I had missed out on Gordon's days up front for Hibs and hadn't appreciated the niftier side of his play.

Our good run in the league continued and we met Celtic just before the share issue at Hibs. It couldn't have happened at a better time for the club and David Duff and Jim Gray obviously thought all their plans for Hibs were on course. It was also Roughie's first time back at Easter Road since he joined Celtic and we had a good crack before the game as usual. That day Roughie saved Celtic from losing six or seven, but everyone just remembers the three he let in.

However, it could have been a lot different as Frank McAvennie broke through in the opening minutes and was brought down by Alan Sneddon. Everybody in the stadium except the referee thought it was a penalty. We then went straight up the pitch to score one, then another and were back in the driving seat. Archie scored two that day and silenced any doubters there were about him being a good buy.

Confidence was now sky high at the club and with the supposed success of the £2 million share flotation we were eagerly awaiting further signings to strengthen the squad. We could compete with the best and knew it. Looking back I'll never forget hearing directors speaking about 'we' when we were doing well, but when we struggled later on I heard the same people say 'they' were rubbish today. It's something you don't forget. In time the atmosphere would deteriorate over the season, especially when they bought pubs instead of players. Our confidence would be seriously undermined. Most players accept financial decisions are the directors' remit, but we all began to think: what's happening here? We haven't even qualified for Europe yet. Surely the priorities were all wrong.

But we were still on a high when we met Manchester United for Gordon Rae's testimonial game, but it's a game I'd rather forget as it is the worst I have played for Hibs. Before the game Alex Miller had told us to treat it like a normal match, but Joe Tortolano took him too seriously and almost put Gordon Strachan into the top tier of the stand early on. I thought the referee might have had a word with the bench, suggesting they substitute Joe, but off he went. We lost 3-0 and I felt bad about it for a couple of days later. Jim Leighton was playing for United and Andy Roxburgh was watching, which added to my anger with myself.

I had just clocked up my first year with Hibs and overall I was pleased how things had gone. I'd played in 52 games and had 25 shut-outs. We had finished sixth in the league and were doing well now. I had also worked myself back into the Scotland squad. Not only that, I was about to play in the World Cup qualifying match against Yugoslavia. So my stinker against Manchester United had not totally blown my chances. Meanwhile we lost our first league game away to Dundee and slipped again, losing to Rangers at home, but then picked up points against Hamilton Accies and Motherwell.

I had been selected for the squad against Yugoslavia not knowing Jim Leighton had picked up an elbow injury. You never

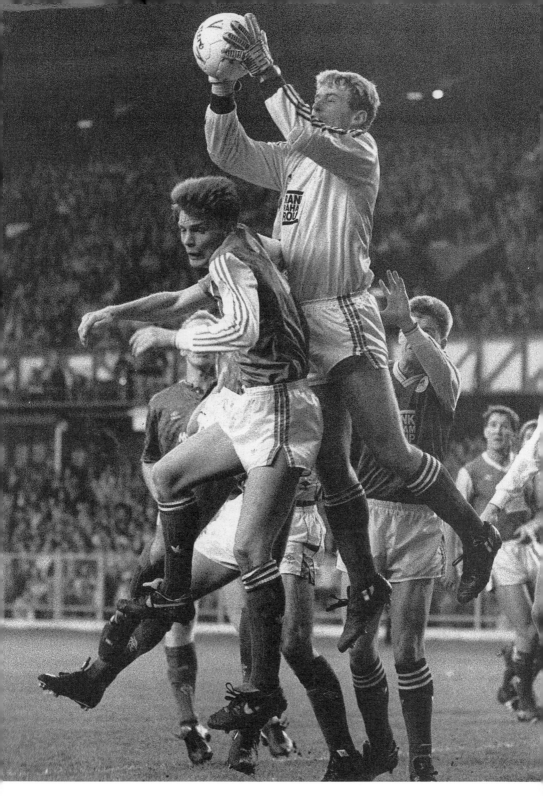

Gordon Hunter is no slouch either, but here he leaves the ball to me.

like to see a teammate injured, but I kidded on Jim, who has been my Scotland roommate for five years, that I had my voodoo doll out sticking pins in it. I was desperate that night to keep a clean sheet and was frustrated by the goal we let in.

The corner they scored from should not have been awarded in the first place and when it came over we really messed it up. It wasn't cleared properly and the shot took a deflection off Paul McStay.

The draw was a disappointment although we hadn't lost. Andy Roxburgh was quoted in the press as saying the most pleasing aspect of the game was the way I played. Well, I can tell you there was no one more pleased than myself. There is nothing better than international football, and returning to league football after it is a bit of a comedown. It's the same after European competition.

Hibs dropped a few more important points at home, drawing 1-1 with Dundee United and losing 2-1 to Aberdeen. Archie scored for us, but again Charlie Nicholas was on target and this time he stuck one in with his backside.

However, the exact pick-me-up we needed was just round the corner. Though things didn't look good at the start of the derby at Tynecastle when Gordon Rae was sent off after ten minutes. The way we fought back and the fact it was a derby make that result one of the most satisfying we have had since I've been at Hibs. Tom MacIntyre switched into the middle of the defence and went on to play his best game for the club. It's terrible if you lose a derby as you have to go into hibernation for the next week if you do so. But since I had arrived we still hadn't lost to Hearts. We won 2-1 with Kano and Archie scoring.

Our form, though, had become inconsistent and we crashed to a disastrous 4-1 defeat at Tannadice.

In December I got another Scotland cap, this time against Italy. The 2-0 defeat in Perugia was a bit of a lesson for us, but I enjoyed it as I had plenty to do. It was also great to revel in the international atmosphere again.

But Hibs were never to recover their early season form although we beat Hearts again in the New Year derby with Eddie May getting the only goal. It seemed then I had a jinx on Hearts, but unfortunately it wasn't to last. It's funny how it works out as Jim McArthur never lost to Hearts, whereas Alan Rough was never on a winning side against them. Three days later Aberdeen beat us 2-0 with, you've guessed it, Charlie Nicholas scoring again. This time he nutmegged me. We bounced back against Dundee, but then any football disappointments I had had were put into perspective when my father died that January.

I knew he had been struggling with chronic bronchitis for some time, but didn't realise the extent of it. Smoking was one of his main pleasures and even if he had stopped just recently, he was so far gone it still would have been too late. My mother phoned me to tell me my father had gone into hospital, but she didn't want me to worry as I had a game with Celtic coming up.

That was typical of them as they tried to give me as few worries as possible so I could get on with my football. I phoned the hospital, but they wouldn't tell me anything over the phone. That night my wife phoned from Bury and said she thought I had better get down there as my parents were not wanting to bother me till after the big game.

When I arrived he was in a ward with ten others and it was clear he wouldn't last long. I asked for a single room as I didn't want everyone in the ward to watch him die.

I wouldn't want anybody to have to go through what I went through that night with my father. My mother left us alone and we had a good cry together. Then he turned to me and said, 'I'm not going to make it.' This was when my mother was still out of the room. I said, 'If you do or you don't it's up to the big one up there.' It got worse and worse as I sat there waiting for him to die. I had always thought of myself as quite a strong character with nothing really phasing me, but that night I cried my eyes out.

At one stage he started breathing easier and he had a wee grin on his face. For a minute I thought the old man was going to pull through. At 7am a nurse came and we were just going to wash him. Three people in his original ward knew him from his footballing days and were asking me about him when I was called back just in time for his last breath.

I cried my eyes out. It was the worst thing I have ever been through.

I have always wished my father had lived to see me get my Scotland cap at cricket just as he had witnessed my other achievements. I was an only child and he had idolised me, but I also idolised him. As a kid he taught me to play football and spent hours teaching me snooker. He was not disliked by anybody. He was just one of those guys who had a nice word for everyone. I travelled up deeply depressed to play Celtic, and bang on 7pm on the Friday the phone went. My father used to phone me every Friday at that time to wish me well and just talk over the game. It was my mother on the phone. I only realised later she was trying to take the place of my father as she rang me usually during the week. That got to me as there she was down in Lancashire on her own completely gutted, and here she was trying to keep me going. It took me a while to get over my father's death and I'm not ashamed to admit I would sometimes go home to cry at night.

To a large extent Joe Royle has stepped into my father's shoes. Whereas I used to phone up my father for advice, I now ring Joe. Joe Royle has always been there and I totally respect him. One time I really felt awful about Joe was when I was set up in a press article which was headlined 'Why I Hated Joe Royle.' I couldn't believe it and immediately got on the phone to him. What I had said had been totally taken out of context. I had been telling the reporter how much I thought of Joe and mentioned I did hate him for a while when he forced me to lose weight at Oldham. I felt awful about the way the article twisted my true opinion of Joe.

Probably I should not have played against Celtic after my father's death, but I did and we lost 3-1. Our form continued to falter, but the highlights for the rest of the season were the cup run, qualifying for Europe and the World Cup games.

Scotland's game in Cyprus was nerve-wracking and no one will forget the jubilation on the bench when Richard Gough made it 3-2 in the final seconds. The night at Hampden a month later when we beat France 2-0 will rate as the greatest atmosphere ever. The hairs on the back of my neck were standing up that night as the Hampden roar urged Scotland on to victory.

Meanwhile in the cup we beat Brechin, Alloa and Motherwell but our cup run was far from convincing. I picked up a personal honour from the Hibs Kids' club for goal of the season thanks to my effort against Morton.

Nice one, Cobber! Jim Gray and Ian McCollie present me with an award from fans 'Down Under'.

Hibs moved into the transfer market again to sign Keith Houchen to strengthen the attack. Everyone knew him from his famous cup-final goal for Coventry. Keith was to get quite a shock when he arrived in Scotland, as most English players do. In the game soon after against Celtic, Mick McCarthy really sorted him out. Keith didn't realise you could get away with that sort of stuff in Scotland and it took him a while to adapt to the physical side of the game. Houch, though, soon settled in and is a buoyant big character who spices up the dressing room with his banter and is a great man for a song.

He scored a great header against Hearts in his debut, but we blew our chances that day. I knew that sometime we would get beaten by Hearts as the longer an unbeaten run goes on, the chances of it coming to an end increase.

Hearts are a team who will always give you a game. They may not be the greatest team going, but they're workmanlike and will die for each other. They have good players in the right positions and tremendous team spirit.

Although Hearts have never splashed out on really big buys, they have spent more than Hibs in recent years. That's why they got back into Europe the following season and Hibs didn't.

We lost again to Aberdeen, which was not the best build-up for the cup semi-final against Celtic. It was played on a Sunday for television and the day before Paul Kane, Gordon Rae and myself were watching television in our hotel. News flashes started coming over from Hillsborough and it soon dawned on us something terrible had happened. Everyone was affected by it, but the next day we had to wipe it out of our minds before the game.

Our cup run had not been that good but I felt some players were due a good game. Against Celtic you know they're going to come at you in the first 20 minutes and try to give you a doing. If you hold them, you then have a chance as if there is no early goal the crowd will get impatient. However, I still feel we didn't freeze that day. It was just we lost such an early goal. Everyone was man-to-man marking when all of a sudden Mick McCarthy gets a free header after three minutes. It was an uphill battle after that as everything came off for Celtic. After their third goal we made a substitution and from then on I thought we were the better team. Archie scored, but we missed other chances. When you play Celtic you know they will never sit on one goal. They are the most attacking team in Scotland, but it can be their undoing at times. In the past teams were happy to win 5-4 but now no manager will risk it.

Anyway the result proved the old adage that losing in the semi-final is worse than losing a final. But the way we lost stung. We never competed in the first half. All the trouble was coming down Tom MacIntyre's side at full back, but I feel he was being overloaded. Celtic outwitted us tactically and by the time we switched things round we were beaten. It was the closest I had come to winning something and I found it very frustrating.

But the season was far from finished as we still had a chance to qualify for Europe a few days later when we played St Mirren at home. We beat them 1-0 thanks to an Archie goal. I had a couple of late saves to make but we were through. There was a lot of tension before that game as we felt we deserved something from the season and the celebrations that night were a real relief.

A class act: Paul McStay and John Collins join me for the Hibs Kids Awards.

There was now a buzz again at Easter Road with the return of European football. Everything had been on the ascent at the club since I had arrived despite some setbacks. Archie and Houch had strengthened us up front, but I don't think people realise what a good team achievement it was as we were far from being a great side. We had a lot of injuries and regularly changed the team around, but hard graft had got us through on many occasions.

For once I couldn't wait for the first day of the pre-season to arrive. Part of the reason I had joined Hibs was to get the chance to play in Europe.

What had made it even better was that Hearts had failed to qualify and all the attention in Edinburgh was on us. The Hibs fans had had to take a lot of stick from Hearts fans in recent years, but we were the top team in the capital once again. I was really pleased for the fans as it gave them something to shout about. Now was the time for the club to strengthen the squad because if we had a few injuries we would be very vulnerable.

We were going into Europe with the bare minimum, but Hibs were back after more than a decade.

CHAPTER SIX

The Willow Wand

I have one secret that I feel I should come clean about. It concerns my abiding passion, something I care about more than football. I'm talking about the greatest game on earth — cricket. I know a lot of Scots will be taken aback by what I have just said but, if I am really honest, I must admit deep down I would have preferred to be a cricketer than a footballer. I know in some ways I have managed to achieve both, but football is my profession and dominates my life. I love cricket, but it is not my livelihood. However, I have no reason to complain because I have been able to combine them. Ironically it was through coming to play football in Scotland that I achieved my ultimate cricketing dream — an international cricket cap, something I would never have got if I had stayed in England.

It was a great honour to become the first man to play football and cricket for Scotland for more than fifty years as the last person to do was Scot Symon, the famous Rangers' manager, who took a memorable 5 for 38 against Bradman's Australians in 1938. In the summer of '89 I represented Scotland at cricket three times and my great pride was only tinged with sadness that my father had not lived to see it.

My passion for cricket arose indirectly through him at the Walshaw Sports Club in Lancashire where he was a steward. There was a South African professional at the club, Goolam Abed, who taught me the basics as I was always hanging around. Through Goolam I got to play for the club's juniors before

Four runs for me against Australia. Aussie Tim May does not look too concerned.

graduating to the Saddleworth League. I had begun to make a name for myself as a schoolboy and got a trial for Lancashire Schools at Old Trafford where I hit 70 runs.

I must have made an impression because I was made captain and played well in my first game against Essex schools. In the next game the England selectors came to take a look at me, but I should have sensed this was not to be my day as we got lost on the 200-mile round trip to Durham and arrived late. Never mind, I thought, I'll soon make up for this as I strode out to open the batting. A minute later I was on my way back to the pavilion after being bowled second ball. That was the end of my England career, but I signed forms with Lancashire Cricket Club which kept my hopes alive.

I was registered with them for four years and relished the experience. Clive Lloyd was kingpin at the club while I played in the thirds with lads who went on to make it like Graham Fowler, Paul Allot and Peter Lee. I like to think I could have made it as a cricketer, but in the end I progressed a lot quicker as a footballer. You also had a chance of making a better living as a footballer, but if I didn't make it in football I believed I could still fall back on cricket.

When I joined Oldham I played every summer in the Saddleworth League with East Lancashire Paper Mill and Mooreside. Dave McCheyne at East Lancs had taught me the ins and outs of the league when I first started playing in a men's league while still a schoolboy. When I was at Mooreside Mike Richardson, a character you either loved or hated, supplied me with all my gear from his Romida shop.

As is fitting for all us crazy goalkeepers, I have a little quirk that I carried over into cricket. I am right-handed at nearly everything I do except cricket. I write with my right hand and feel more comfortable saving with my right in goal, but as a lad I had a left-handed grip when I played golf. My father had only right-handed clubs, but I adapted to using them with a left-handed grip. When I started playing cricket I also adopted a left-handed grip with my bat. I can't really explain why I did it, because as I said, as a goalie I throw out and punch with my right. Call me an oddball, but it's just one of those things.

When I joined Hibs there was an article in the paper which said I'd played for Lancashire at cricket and it aroused the interest of a few local clubs. The first club to approach me was Penicuik, so I started playing for them. Some of the others offered me quite a few quid to play for them, but I turned them down as I felt I should be loyal to Penicuik. They were first in for me and had treated me well. If I stayed with them I was told I had a chance of getting a Scotland B cap. They were also a great bunch of lads who treated me as one of them, not Andy Goram the footballer.

I had played in a few district games when one of the Penicuik committee took me aside and told me I had been picked for

Scotland. I initially thought he meant the B team until he explained it would be against Yorkshire in the Nat West Trophy at Headingley. I needed no encouragement as it would be the War of the Roses for a Lancashire lad like me. We went to Yorkshire and were a bit unlucky to lose, but I had a fabulous time. On the first day play was rained off early so I went to the Ladbrokes tent with Dave Cowan to have a bet on the racing. After half an hour a message came over the tannoy that play would not resume today. We stayed in the tent for the rest of the afternoon and had a great time, winning about £300 each. After we had changed in the dressing room we went on to the National Westminster's hospitality tent for a drink. I could not believe the difference between cricket and football. There was none of the strictness associated with football and we all relaxed, players and management together having a good few drinks. Of course I appreciate football is a professional sport and most of the Scotland cricketers were amateurs, so the management don't have the same hold on them. As long as you do the business out there on the pitch it doesn't matter what you do off it as long as you don't go over the score. Even the Yorkshire players had a few pints that night although they were playing the next day.

When I was picked to play Yorkshire, I explained to the Scotland selectors if they considered me again I might have difficulties because of my commitments to Hibs. I thought they might leave me out but I was picked again to play in a three-day game against Ireland in Dublin. I went to see Hibs boss Alex Miller who was as straight as ever and said it was alright, but this was the last time. I had no idea then I would be picked again to play Australia. The trip to Ireland turned out to be the best I have ever had with a team and the Irish hospitality lived up to everything I had ever heard about it.

I knew Oman Henry, the guru of Scottish cricket from the Saddleworth league, and he more than welcomed me to the team. He always referred to me as 'Hibs', never Andy, which caught on among the other lads. On the last day the match finished at 4.30pm and we were rushing to get ready afterwards as we were due to fly back at 6pm. One of the selectors came into the dressing room looking very solemn and announced he had some bad news for us. The flight time on the tickets was wrong and we had missed the flight so we would have to stay another night. The place erupted in the biggest cheer of the last three days. We were delighted at the thought of another night in Dublin and it turned out to be the best of the lot so far.

I had one experience there which I thought could only happen in Ireland. I was coming in for my third ball bowling when this wee Irish umpire turns to me and says, 'Maurice Johnston has just signed for Rangers.' I took a double take. 'What's that, wee man?' 'Maurice Johnston has signed for Rangers.' Here I am a Lancashire lad playing for Scotland in Ireland and Maurice Johnston has just signed for Rangers. He had been a Celtic player when we had left Scotland. Next ball I was hit for six as I had completely lost the place. 'This can't be real.' Sure enough when we came off I found it was true and I must say it was a brilliant move. Graeme Souness had got to be applauded for signing a Catholic. Whatever you say about Souness, you have to admit he was probably the only manager brave enough to do it and it was hardly as if he was signing a bad Catholic. He had got one of the best no matter what religion he was.

Alex Miller had been clear that the Ireland game was to be my last as we were now into pre-season training. The chairman of the Scotland selectors then contacted me and asked if I'd like to play against Australia. I told him that I wasn't supposed to, but of course I'd be honoured to play. It would be a dream come true. For any cricketer, playing Australia is equivalent to Scotland playing Brazil at football.

I went to training at Easter Road and told Alex Miller I had been picked and he, Peter Cormack and I sat down on the grass after training to discuss it. Alex said he didn't want me to play and if I did I would have to face the consequences. But he added he thought he knew what I was going to do anyway.

Here was my chance to play against the team who had just won the Ashes, possibly the best team in the world. I couldn't miss this game. It's what every cricket fan dreams of. It wasn't a case of me being a rebel and going against my club. It was just something I had to do.

Once the news got out that I was playing, the press soon got hot

One regret is my father never lived to see me get a cap for Scotland at cricket.

on my trail, blowing up the clash between me and Hibs. Alex Miller did not want me to risk injury, and Jim Gray was quoted in the press: 'If Andy gets injured it will not be a cricketer getting injured, but a silly footballer getting injured.' I take his point. Looking back I can see why some people might have thought I was a bit daft, but I had a lot more chance of getting injured with Penicuik and the pitches they played on than on a top-class pitch in an international.

Nothing was going to stop me no matter how high the fine was. I think Hibs were maybe pressurised into taking a stand because with the season about to start people might have been saying Hibs' keeper was taking unnecessary risks. Also some would say I should just concentrate on football as that's what I'm paid to do. In Scotland there not the same tradition there is down south where Denis Compton is the most famous example of someone who was both a top-class footballer and cricketer.

However, I felt Hibs could have turned the whole situation to their advantage and use it as a public relations exercise. After all I was the first man to earn a double cap in cricket and football for Scotland in fifty years. I was also the first player to be fined for playing for his country.

Despite the flak I was taking I got a lot of support from cricket people. Before the game the Australian manager Bobby Simpson told me he thought I was doing the right thing and everyone in cricket was right behind me. Alan Border, the Australian captain, said he couldn't believe my club would fine me and I was getting all this trouble for playing for my country. Alan wished me all the best and told me to go out and enjoy it.

It was a great day at Hamilton Crescent with a crowd of about 4-5,000. When I turned up for nets at 10am the press were already there trying to get me to say something that would wind up the situation with Hibs. I was saying nothing and was keen to get on with it. I don't think I did too badly that day as I bowled a bit and scored four runs.

When I went into bat I got a great reception. The crowd were right behind me because I had gone against my club and taken a stand. But all that soon went out the window as I faced up to Merv Hughes. He's a big aggressive fellow. I took one look at him and thought, blimey, he could do me a lot of damage. He may not look quite as quick as some of the West Indians, but I can assure you he is bloody fast. As I waited at the crease I saw him taking this huge run up, but thought surely he won't drop one short on me first ball. So to get off to a start I started moving forward, which was a mistake as, to put it lightly, he gave me one hell of a bouncer. I realised half way forward that he had dropped it short and tried to get out of the way but the ball just followed me. It went whizzing past my helmet and splattered into the wicket-keeper's gloves. I looked back up at him and he was halfway down the wicket. He glowered at me, fingering his moustache and snapped, 'Stick to football, son.'

I thought, 'What have I gone and let myself in for?' Getting battered about on a football pitch was better than this any day. I still don't know how I survived that over, but he is the fastest thing I have ever faced.

But the Aussies were not all about intimidation. They sent a massive cooler full of beer into our dressing room. We were a wee bit wary as we thought they were trying to get us drunk. We had got off to a great start and were 90 for 1 and still thought we had a bit of a chance. So only two cans were drunk during the game. After the match I went into see one of the Aussies I knew from the Lancashire league and get a bat autographed. I looked into their cooler and there was only one can left. Here we were thinking they were taking the game seriously, but they had been playing when they were half cut. They were only here for the beer. It was an exhibition game for them, but for us lot it was the biggest game of our lives.

As usual the camaraderie after the game was top class and there was a dinner in Glasgow City Chambers for both teams. I never regretted what I'd done for a minute. I didn't seek a public confrontation with Hibs, but as I've said it was just something I could not turn down. I had achieved another one of my ambitions in life. I duly paid my fine from Hibs, but can tell you it was nothing like the £2,000 quoted in the press.

CHAPTER SEVEN

Back to Where We Once Belonged

Not only must I be the first player to be fined for playing for his country, but I must be one of the few who are fined one minute and offered the club captaincy the next. With the cricket season behind me I was really looking forward to the football season, and the offer of the captain's armband added an extra interest. It would be a test, but I felt I was up to it.

Maybe I was offered it to make up for the cricket fine, as I think deep down the management understood my decision, but felt they had to be seen to be taking a stand. Anyway Gordon Rae was injured and not many of the other players really fancied the job. Neil Cooper could have been a contender but he had just arrived at Easter Road. Peter Cormack said the team needed a strong personality and, to be honest, I pushed myself into the job. I asked the manager to give me a shot and he was willing to take a chance. He said we'd see how it went and so far it seems to have gone not too badly.

A lot of people think a keeper is not the ideal player to be captain but as long as you lead by example I think you're doing your job. The captain has to be a player his team-mates look up to. Whether they look up to me at Easter Road is not for me to say. My ideal example of the captain who leads by example is Roy Aitken. He held Celtic together for so many seasons and has inspired Scotland on numerous occasions. Only people who do not really understand football criticise Roy. Ask anyone in the game what they think of the big man and they'll soon set you straight.

I was a bit apprehensive about stepping into Gordon Rae's shoes as he had done a great job as captain. My first season as captain would be the hardest, but I knew I would learn. Hibs are a quiet young team and the squad had never tended to socialise off the park. I saw it as my job to help create a team spirit and sort things out for the lads off the pitch. I organised a few social occasions to try and weld us together. The more you know a guy, the more you will stick by him on the pitch. At the end of the day I go on and toss the coin and wear an armband. I can shout and scream and tell them how things should be going, but if the ten others do the same, you don't really need a captain. Or rather you should have another ten captains on the pitch.

Despite the honour of being club captain, my relations with the club were beginning to strain. I had won a pre-season holiday to Hawaii as the Legal and General's Hibs Player of the Year. It was a superb holiday and something I'll always remember. Trophies are nice to get, but really all you can do with them is stick them in your cabinet. Hawaii, though, was a once-in-a-lifetime experience.

Just before I went my agent at the time asked for a new contract from Hibs. Alex Miller said the club would be bankrupt if they met my demands. Then the day I left for Hawaii Jim Gray slaughtered me in the press for being greedy. I resented that as he knew fine well there was no way I could answer back as I would be sunning myself in the South Seas. I thought it was a fair demand I had put in. I don't think most people would believe what I was actually getting paid when I first came to Hibs. Less than a year later I asked for more than that offer and Hibs agreed to it. I was two minutes away from signing the new contract but we couldn't agree on the length of it. I wanted a three-year extension to my present contract, but Hibs would only offer a one-year extension.

But at this time the club accused me of being greedy and trying to bankrupt them. Yet nine months later they were prepared to offer me more. It made me wonder what they were really up to!

I didn't see Jim Gray's remarks until I got back from Hawaii. To say the least, I wasn't pleased. The club also said I had enhanced my reputation as an international by playing for Hibs. At that time, though, I had got more Scottish caps playing with Oldham. Also I disagreed with their inference that they had made me into the goalie I am now. Hibs had done nothing special for me as a keeper with their training or taught me anything new. Hibs had given me the opportunity to play at a higher level and that gave me the opportunity to improve as a player. I will always appreciate that, but it was Alan Hodgkinson and Joe Royle who made me the player I am today. I also like to think I had helped Hibs since my arrival at the club.

Unfortunately, I wasn't the only one having problems with the club. Steve Archibald's clashes with the management began to surface in the press. Archie's comment that Hibs were a small-time club was countered by Jim Gray's assertion that he had a big-club contract. Archie had played with Tottenham and Barcelona and knew what he was talking about. We all realised Hibs had the potential to be big-time and they had a great tradition, but in recent years the club had been badly run. The revival since the new board took over had been a boost, but we were beginning to have our reservations. I was still the club's highest signing at just over £300,000, which spoke for itself. When Archie left later on in the season it was the biggest loss Hibs had suffered since I had joined them. However, worse was to come later on. Meanwhile Alex Miller had reshuffled the pool with a limited budget. Eddie May, a player I personally rated, was transferred to Brentford and Brian Hamilton and Neil Cooper were signed from the boss's old club. Neil Cooper is probably one of the best value-for-money signings Hibs have made. He cost only £30,000 but has played like a half-million-pound player. He took over from Gordon Rae, and it's indicative of how well he played that Gordon couldn't win his place back. Brian Hamilton, however, got off to a difficult start. The fans got on his back right away, which made matters worse. At times you could see Brian was very depressed at training, but full credit to him as he stuck in there and had begun to prove his critics wrong by the end of the season. Just as he was hitting top form he broke his leg at Ibrox. I believe the fans have been unfair to Brian. Some players are lucky when they move as they settle in immediately. Others flatter to deceive at first and end up not fulfilling their early promise. You're better off with a stayer any day.

We got off to a flying start in the League and despite growing

Being club captain meant more responsibility but that didn't bother me. Here I'm probably more worried about who won the 3.30 at Doncaster.

problems felt confident. We beat Rangers in our first game at Easter Road. It was Bonni Ginzberg's league debut and we had decided to put him under pressure. The Premier League was obviously a lot different from what he was used to. It was also one of those days when the weather was a factor. Before the game the boss and I decided if we won the toss we would go against the wind and try and get in at half-time 0-0. In the second half we would blitz them and they would also be running uphill against the wind.

Winning the toss won us the game, as everything went to plan with the added bonus of Keith Houchen sneaking a goal in the first half. Bonni Ginzberg took a bit of stick for the second, dropping a cross that Mickey Weir stuck in. We ran out comfortable winners and I thoroughly enjoyed myself, twice coming out the box to play sweeper. One of the times I actually dribbled round Ally McCoist before passing upfield.

But our next game should have told us what sort of a season we would have — more than competing with the best but toiling against lesser opponents. We faced Clydebank in the Skol Cup at Easter Road and it turned out one of those nights where we had everything to lose.

They took us to extra time and the boss came on to sort out the penalty-takers. He asked who wanted to take one and I was first with my hand up. Again this was because it was something I had always wanted to do so I could look back on my career and say I had done it. Also I thought as captain I shouldn't shirk responsibility.

They missed their fourth penalty and I went up to place the ball. George Stewart told me later he had been watching the players in the centre spot and turned to his mate in the stand and said, 'Look, none of them wants to take it'. His mate nudged him and says, 'Take a look at the penalty spot'. There I was plonking the ball down. I could feel the stir in the crowd as no one was expecting me to take it.

Jim Gallacher looked about 7ft in goal. As I took my run-up it did cross my mind I might not have been doing the right thing. If I missed I would take some stick. But I had decided which way to put it and in it went. I couldn't have scripted it better myself.

The season continued to stutter along and we lost 1-0 to Hearts with Musemic scoring. Before the game we had decided to watch him at set pieces in the air. That was his strength as we didn't rate him on the deck. For all our good intentions. who but Musemic should get a free header at a free kick and stick it in?

However, the prospect of European football kept us all buoyant.

When we had first heard the draw it had been a case of Video-who? When the big night arrived it was the most nervous the team had been for a long time. For most of us it was our first European game. It was also a special night for the fans as it was Hibs' first European tie since they played Strasbourg in 1978.

The crowd that night were terrific and got right behind us. But despite plenty of pressure we didn't take our chances in front of goal. When we did score it was thanks to the eccentricity foreign keepers are renowned for. Their keeper Zsolt Petry punched out a cross he should have caught. It went straight to Neil Orr who fired in a shot which Graeme Mitchell deflected with his head into the net. Most of the press felt we hadn't done enough to get through, but we felt we could handle their forwards in Hungary and we would also have a lot more room.

Our European euphoria was short-lived when we were knocked out of the League Cup 3-1 at home by Dunfermline. As if that wasn't bad enough, I had to take something I have never seen in football before. The club programme had a go at me. As I said, it was the first time I had come across a player getting stick in the club programme. I had always thought it stood behind you no matter what.

Despite that setback we were third in the table mid-October. There was a buzz around the club and Alex Miller was quoted in the press saying I had become an even bigger inspiration since I had become captain. The new challenge had given me responsibility. I enjoyed it and it showed in my game. In ten matches I had only let in three goals.

As we set off for the return tie with Videoton we were quietly confident and determined to get everything out of the experience. On the trip over I decided to get the boys relaxed and give them a laugh by dressing up as an air hostess with lipstick, blusher and the full gear on. I won't reveal if I was wearing suspenders or not. It went down a treat and set the buoyant mood that stayed with us throughout the trip.

The night before the boss took me on my own for one of the best training sessions I had had for a long time.

Everything went perfectly. I was catching everything he fired at me. The afternoon before the game was like the lull before the storm. We were sent to bed to rest. I always room with Paul Kane, which is an education in itself. Kano has a vast fund of stories about Hibs. I'm sure he knows more about the club than it does itself. As we were in our room Kano calls me over as there's this hubbub down below our room on a patio. As we looked over there was David Duff, Jim Gray and Raymond Sparkes with a group of fans and some of the Videoton people having a laugh. I'll never forget the sight of big Frank Dougan, Hibs' most famous fan, sitting on a wee swing chair. Every time it creaked Kano and I increased the odds on it going. We spent the rest of the afternoon relaxing by watching them have a good time.

Come the game we were confident our good defensive record would stand us in good stead. Early on I got down well to a 30-yard shot. It was my first touch and I was happy, but it wasn't as if I would have much to do. We were soon one up. Graeme Mitchell went down the left and crossed for Keith Houchen to stick it in with his head. That goal had more or less won us the game as they had to score three now. We went in 1-0 at half-time and there was chaos in the dressing room. Everyone was shouting and yelling at the same time, we were so high. We were almost verging on hysteria. The boss quietened us down and told us to make sure we kept it tight and we would get another. Less than 15 minutes into the second half Gareth Evans made it two and then the rough stuff started. We were expecting it as in the first leg at Easter Road they had been flinging it about and Mickey Weir and Quiriko should have been sent off in the closing stages. Tomas Petres, who was their best player, cracked and elbowed Neil Cooper in the face off the ball. I came out of my goal to see how Neil was and had forgotten the ball was still in play. The referee had now spotted the incident and sent Petres off. We kept our cool despite more provocation and played some of the best football of any team I've been in. Johnnie Collins made it 3-0 and we coasted home. Our passing had been superb. From the final whistle it was celebrations all night.

As we were leaving the stadium I asked the boss if we could have a few beers on the bus. Normally he never allows it, but as this was a special occasion he permitted it. I spotted Billy Erskine, a Powderhall bookie, and asked him to get some bevy. Meanwhile

Chris Reid, my understudy at Hibs, is a great prospect.

the singing continued and the bus set off for the hotel. Just then I caught sight of a little figure arms full of wine bottles running after the bus screaming at us. Of course it was Billy whom we had clean forgotten about in the euphoria. Here we had almost gone and left behind the main man. We sang Hibs songs all the way back. Alan Sneddon, who had played in Europe with Celtic, said this was a night to top them all. It was the best away result he had ever seen. A lot of the press agreed, saying it was one of the best away results by a Scottish club for a long time.

All credit to Videoton as their full team turned up for the dinner afterwards in the hotel and stayed while we were singing, laughing and joking throughout the meal.

Gordon Hunter, who never usually drinks, took a glass of

champagne I offered him. Afterwards he and I were first into the bar and I ordered another ten bottles of champagne. Somehow the others got delayed as Gordon and I waited on our own. Every ten minutes or so I noticed he was getting more and more drunk as the champagne began to disappear. Then it was as if he had hit a brick wall. He couldn't speak so I thought I had better get him back to the hotel. I got him out of the bar and had to carry him back to the hotel. He was singing all kinds of Hibs songs and saying how much he loved Hibs. He was also paralytic. It is probably the best night Gordon's had and definitely the worst he has ever felt the next morning. I put him to bed and he was ill everywhere. But it was just that kind of night when even a teetotaller hit the bevy.

Back in the Premier League we were a bit drained by our European excursion and drew 2-2 with Dunfermline at home. We had lost eight goals so far and five of them had been to Dunfermline. Again I was playing sweeper. Anything that comes over the top I usually move for, so when a long ball came through I started to come out. I had gone 10 yards and had another 15 to go and thought I might not make it, but kept going. I headed the ball forward to set John Collins off on the move he would score from.

Alex Miller won the Manager of the Month award, which was a reflection on how well we were doing. My spirits were high and reports of West Ham's interest in me were just a compliment. It didn't unsettle me because as far as I was concerned I would be staying at Hibs. I didn't think they would want to sell me and I was happy with things as they were. The press also started touting me for a Scotland place in the forthcoming World Cup game against France. Jim Leighton had taken a lot of stick for the débâcle in Zagreb a few weeks earlier. However, I thought Andy Roxburgh would stick by Jim, but I took it as a compliment to have the press pushing my name.

Once again Scotland hit rock bottom, this time in Paris with a 3-0 defeat. However, I was picked up by a 3-2 League win over Motherwell the following Saturday. My old pal Steve Kirk got in a sneaky one in that game when he sent me crashing to the ground. Obviously he was still smarting from the time I laughed in his face after saving his penalty. My close encounters with him are the only reason I and the fans look forward to the Motherwell game.

By now we were ready to meet Liège at home in the next round of the UEFA Cup. We realised it would be harder than Videoton but with a brilliant atmosphere at Easter Road we were confident. We couldn't have asked for a better start as we got an early penalty. As Keith Houchen placed the ball there was a long delay, because Alan Sneddon had gone over on his ankle. Keith changed his mind which way he was putting it during the delay and Munaron, their keeper, saved it.

Usually Kano took them, but you always have a back-up just in case that player is injured or badly off form. Alex Miller had left it to Kano and Keith to decide. I think Keith was the right man on the night to take it. He had scored against Videoton and the Saturday before against Motherwell. He was the form player. Snoddy's injury delay was crucial and it was a great save rather than a poor miss. We were disappointed by our failure to score at home and our League form slumped with 3-0 defeats to both Aberdeen and Rangers. We were to lose 13 goals in five League games, which was a turn round after our defensive record had been so good. The team began to get switched about, and as soon as we were knocked out of Europe by Liège our season was turned upside down. From being second or third in the League we found we couldn't get a result anywhere.

I had noticed it happened to Hearts the season before. They had some good results in Europe, but their League form suffered. I didn't understand it at the time as I hadn't been in Europe, but now I can. It's a real comedown returning to the Premier League after European football. You get great games in Europe with a totally different kind of football, but at home it's a war of attrition.

However, we didn't go out of Europe with our tails between our legs.

Once again I decided to give the boys a laugh on the way out there and arrived in Belgium with a pair of three-foot-long giant gloves on and a silly mask. Despite our League form we were desperate to do well as we had all loved our European experience so far.

I heard Lou Macari was in Liège to watch me and was going to make a £1 million bid after the game. This did a wee bit extra to keep me on my toes, not that I really needed it. The papers called me 'The Lion of Liège' that night and said 'Even Goram's brilliance could not stop Scotland's last club going out.' I was praised for one particular save off Danny Boffin and a header from Nisskens. But the winning goal was unbelievable.

We had gone into the second half of extra time when they got a corner. We were already thinking about penalties as we had more than contained them. The ball was cleared to their sweeper and skipper De Sart who was 40 yards from goal. Gareth Evans went charging out to him to close him down. All De Sart could do was hit it with his left foot. Gareth had gone out directly in line with me so I couldn't see the shot take off. It had travelled 10 yards before I saw it coming but it was too late for me to get any height off the floor. I heard it hit the bar and as I landed on the deck I turned and saw the ball coming out. I never thought it had gone in so I dived on top of it and turned to put it up the park. It was only then I saw the ref running to the halfway line and realised it must have crossed the line, bouncing down and then out.

I punched the ball to the halfway line. I really felt aggrieved as De Sart hadn't scored for five years. He was also right-footed and here he was knocking it in from 40 yards with his left. If Gareth hadn't closed him down undoubtedly he would have pulled it down and played it. Losing was a real downer. Especially the way they had scored, and the way I played I thought that was one game where I deserved a clean sheet.

There was another thing that frustrated me. The press had reported Steve Archibald was injured and couldn't play, but that was not the case. I think the club put that out just to placate the fans. Why Archie wasn't in the squad I don't know for sure, but I would guess he had had another argument with the management. The next Saturday Archie was fit enough to play against Hearts and scored a cracker. That was typical of Archie — always at the centre of some controversy. I can say most of the team thought Archie should have been taken to Liège. His experience would have been invaluable. He had played in the World Cup and a European Cup final. I still think to this day if Archie had played

The eyes have it. Concentration is vital at all times if you are a keeper.

we would have won in Liêge. When it came to the big occasion
Hibs displayed small-time thinking when they left him at home.
After the Liège game I did myself no favours in our League match
at Tannadice. Andy Roxburgh was there and the World Cup
game against Norway was looming. I still thought it unlikely he
would do something as radical as drop Jim Leighton for the last
qualifying game, but again the pressure was on after the France
game.

The night before I had gone to bed at nine o'clock but I might as
well have been up all night for the way I was caught napping after
five minutes. Maurice Malpas hit a speculative shot from 25 yards.
Often the easy shots are the hardest because your concentration
slips. I took my eye off it for a split second to see where I was going
to throw it, but the ball bounced off my chest and Darren Jackson

stuck it in. The whole place went quiet for a minute as I think the fans were as embarrassed as I was.

Two games later we got our first win in eight games, which again indicates how much we had slipped. We beat Dundee 3-2 but with no thanks to the linesman or referee. I dived to save a Stuart Beedie shot with my back to the linesman, so he couldn't see the ball. Part of my body crossed the line but my arms stayed well out in front, but as I had dived behind the line he must have thought I had crossed it. Stuart Beedie and the Dundee players didn't even appeal and seemed to be taken aback when they saw it was awarded, but they celebrated nonetheless.

After that game I missed my first game since joining Hibs when I went in for an operation on an ulcer on my kneecap. I should have had it seen to earlier, but it wasn't the club that was pushing me. I knew if I missed games my chances of playing for Scotland in the World Cup would be reduced. I should have got my knee done earlier but thought it was something that would go away after a while.

It had been giving me gyp at the end of the previous season, but when I had played cricket all summer I had never felt it. At one stage I didn't train for three weeks, only playing in matches. I put on about a stone in weight and did miss training. I actually enjoy it apart from all the running. Stick me in goal all day and I love it. I also missed the crack with the lads. Chris Reid came in against Dunfermline and had a great game. He is a very good keeper who will make it to the top.

I am not a good spectator and watched the game from the stand. For a couple of incidents I was up off my seat when all of a sudden this Dunfermline fan starts having a go at me. So after a while I started returning the verbal compliments, but realised I had better button it as it wouldn't look too good in the press: Hibs' keeper involved in a brawl. Chris Reid played a blinder that day and probably had the best debut for any keeper I have ever seen.

I went into a private hospital at Murrayfield for my operation. I didn't realise what sort of place it was until the nurse offered me the menu on my first night. It was better than half the restaurants in Edinburgh. I went for glory and had the works. Just as she was leaving, I turned a page and saw the wine list. I asked her if I was allowed something to drink and she said 'Certainly' so I ordered a bottle of Beaujolais. When she came to clear up I got my wrists slapped for asking for another.

I've already admitted I'm a bit squeamish about needles, to put it mildly. Just before the operation they threw me into a right panic when they told me they would operate when I was awake. I'd get an injection but they would cover it up. I would feel them fiddling about but there would be no pain. Captain Courageous was having none of it and they promptly put me under.

I probably came back too early and could have ended up like Theo Snelders, but I was lucky. We went up to Aberdeen and won 2-1, which was another example of our funny season. But we reverted to our poor form, losing the New Year derby 2-0. We had only scored nine goals in our last 21 games, which was a pretty pathetic record, and matters up front were not helped at all when Steve Archibald was dropped for the game against Motherwell.

The boss named the team in the dressing room at Motherwell and left for us to get stripped. Archie was out. The usual procedure is that those not playing go up to the stand for a pie. Archie just looked at me and Paul Kane. He left the room and I turned to Kano and said, 'What's that about, then?' Just then Archie comes in and picks up his bag. We asked him what he was doing. 'Getting out of here. I've ordered a taxi.' We just laughed as we though he was joking but he wasn't. It was another example of his single-mindedness. Once he decided to do something, there's no stopping him.

This was the beginning of the end of Archie's long-running dispute with the club. The atmosphere between the two was to degenerate to the point where it was better that Archie did leave, both for his own sake and the club's. We would sorely miss him and I'm sure the situation could have been handled a lot better. He was ordered to train on his own with the kids. The whole scenario was pathetic and became embarrassing. I think the manager and the board thought Archie was poisoning some of us and criticising the set-up. Archie had assessed the situation for himself and obviously had no faith in the people currently running the club.

We then lost 1-0 to St Mirren at home with a section of the crowd chanting 'Miller must go'. The boss took all the stick whenever we played badly but a lot of fans didn't give him credit when we played well. Soon as there were any problems — 'Miller Must Go.' Whenever we win he puts all the praise onto the team in the press.

Our 2-0 win at Brechin's pokey wee park helped revive the situation and then it was topsy turvy again, losing 2-0 at Dundee and unlucky only to draw 1-1 at Parkhead.

Another boost was winning the Tennents Sixes. There were very good odds on Hibs, so a lot of the boys from my local in Bonnyrigg, The Calderwood, put money on and travelled through to the Scottish Exhibition Centre. I felt we had the right sort of team for the sixes with players like Collins, Kane, McGinlay and Sneddon. Paul Kane once again showed what an all-rounder he was, scoring eight goals.

In the semis we met Hearts which went to a penalty shoot-out. I saved from both John Robertson and Gary Mackay as we got one over on them. As Henry Smith and I passed each other for each kick it might have looked on television as if we were involved in friendly banter, but we were swearing and cursing at each other. 'You'll miss this one you jambo b★★★★★★.' 'F★★★ you, ya Hibbie git.' All nice clean stuff.

We beat St Mirren in the final and I was delighted as it was the first time I had ever won anything at senior level. I know it was only the sixes but it was still a great feeling. I had also let in only two goals in the tournament.

That night about twenty of us celebrated at Gordon's Trattoria in Edinburgh. When you get the managing director's wife dancing on a table, then you know you've had a good night out.

CHAPTER EIGHT

Heading for the Rocks

The Tennents Sixes were the last good thing to happen to Hibs under the former board. From then on problems started popping up all over the place. The disharmony and unhappiness among many of the players were there for everyone to see. The full impact of what was festering underneath would not be exposed for another five months.

Meanwhile we missed out on a player who could well have clinched a place in Europe for us. None of us had heard of Ronnie Rosenthal and few of us saw him play. He came from Standard Liège for a trial in a reserve game at Ibrox and was away again before we knew what was happening. He said he would like to play for Hibs but the terms he wanted were considered too high. In hindsight, a £50,000 signing-on fee didn't seem too much when we saw what he did at Liverpool.

In many ways you can understand the manager's caution when there isn't a lot of money around. But what sickened me and quite a few others was how the club played safe when it came to football, but were the complete opposite when it came to their business investments. Once again it was clear to the players that the priorities were all wrong.

At this time I went in for a new contract with Hibs. Although my contract was not up till autumn 1991 I was asking for a five-year contract. As I've said, money wasn't the problem, but Hibs would only offer me a three-year contract, which meant a one-year extension to what I was on at the time. Words were exchanged between Jim Gray and me in the press. As it wasn't settled, it meant that the matter would drag on and relations between me and the club were up and down.

Not long after that Hibs again displayed a bit of brinkmanship when they said there would be no bargaining over contracts for John Collins, Paul Kane and Gordon Hunter which were all due to expire. There would be no haggling over the offers. They either wanted to play for Hibs or not. If Hibs had come clean about their situation a lot earlier, the players would have understood. As it was, we were kept in the dark.

When my talks had fallen through I said it was clear Hibs didn't have the money. Jim Gray's response was to hit out in the press saying it was a fallacy to say the club had no money as they had just bought Mark McGraw for £200,000. This was followed soon after by £300,000 on Paul Wright. True, it was an outlay by Hibs but it was hardly megabucks. Later events would show that the club was in serious financial trouble. Both the signings, though, were good ones.

It was ironic that we should score our biggest win under Alex Miller — 5-1 against Brechin in the Cup — just before we signed a striker. Despite that result we had been toiling for goals and Paul Wright was a welcome addition. He had scored a few times against us when he was with Aberdeen. It had been said he had a weight problem, but once he was fully fit we were confident he would start sticking them in. In training he immediately showed he liked to have a go. He was very direct and shot at goal instinctively.

It was another piece of bad luck both for him and the club that he was badly injured. He scored the winner in his first game against his old club Aberdeen in a 3-2 home win and looked the man who could make the difference between qualifying for Europe or not.

While we were signing players, Gordon Rae joined Partick Thistle for £65,000. I was very sorry to see him go as I liked Gordon a lot. He had helped me out when I first joined Hibs along with Paul Kane. Gordon was instrumental in me moving to Bonnyrigg when I was having a few problems in Edinburgh. We had also had the best season since I had been at Hibs when Gordon was in the middle of the defence alongside Graeme Mitchell. It was also probably Gordon's best season at the club.

Foiling Wayne Foster of Hearts. My arrival at Hibs helped reverse a ten year spell without a win against our old rivals.

All players know that most of you will move on sometime. It is the old conveyor belt system that is part of the game. We get a good laugh in the dressing room at a lot of the press reports and more often than not you can't believe what they print.

However, Alex Miller had been going out of his way to secure the future of the club by offering a five-year contract to Willie Miller similar to Billy Finlay's. Also Mark McGraw looked a real prospect. But to get success you have to hang onto your senior players and top up the first-team pool with experience.

John Collins had publicly expressed dissatisfaction with the Premier League and we all thought he would be going abroad at the end of the season. Johnnie was rooming next door to me during the World Cup in Italy and we all thought he was heading for Bordeaux. He had even brought a French phrase book with him and told us about their training facilities and the house they were offering him. Then he signed for Celtic and came out with one of the immortal lines in the press: 'I always wanted to play for

Celtic.' If he had gone to Bordeaux Hibs would have lost a lot of money, so it paid the club to sell him off to one of their rivals.

John is a player with exceptional talent and I still think he missed a chance to play in the World Cup. He wasn't happy playing on the left side of midfield at Hibs as he didn't get enough of the ball. A young player like him has no right to dictate to the manager. He should have buckled down and he could have claimed the Scotland spot. He is the best left-sided midfield man Scotland have had for a long time. Part of the reason Scotland lost to Costa Rica in the World Cup was because we did not play with natural wide men in the midfield. If the manager wants you to play somewhere, you have to do it.

An ideal example of a player who will play anywhere for the club is Paul Kane. I am sure he would play in goal if asked to. He has played full back, midfield and striker and done more than an adequate job in all positions. Kano is just that sort of character. It shows off the park, as I'm sure he knows half of Edinburgh. He loves Hibs and the fans know it. When he says he has never driven through Gorgie in his life, I believe him.

The uneven nature of our season continued. We were knocked out of the Cup 1-0 by Dundee United and then went to Ibrox in the League and won 1-0. It was only Rangers' second home defeat of the season. Keith Houchen got our goal and John Collins and Paul Kane were outstanding in midfield. Ibrox has the sort of atmosphere players like Kane and myself love. You're guaranteed a full house and you know Rangers will come at you. Games with them are rarely boring. Going there affects people in different ways. You either rise to the occasion or hide. It was my first League win at Ibrox although we had a few draws there. The only thing that soured it was that Brian Hamilton broke his leg. He was having a brilliant game when he went into a tackle and we heard a crack. I though it was only his shin pad but it was a lot worse. It put a damper on things but we had taken more points off Rangers than anyone else. If we had done it against lesser sides, our season would have turned out a lot different. We were so inconsistent, but at the start of the season I knew we would be in trouble as we didn't have a strong enough pool to withstand injuries.

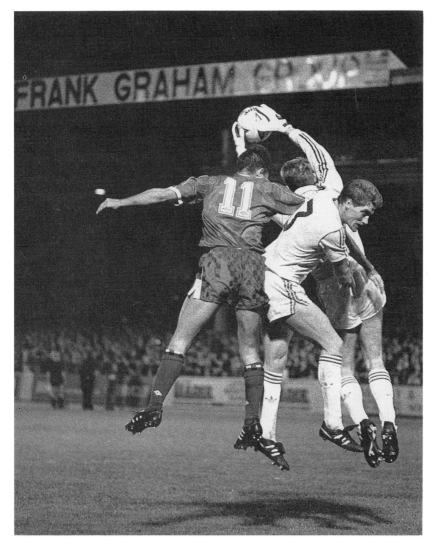

Alan Sneddon rides shotgun as I save against Aberdeen. Wearing white that night Peter Cormack said would make us play like Real Madrid. Aberdeen won 2-1.

Both John Collins and I were selected to play Argentina in the World Cup warm-up at Hampden. It was a big chance for me with the finals approaching. The press were calling for Jim Leighton's head and there were a lot of bad reports on him and United from down south.

I was really keyed to play, plus the fact I had played against Brazil and Italy already. Argentina would have made a nice hat-trick of playing against the greatest teams in the world. Chances like this come along once in a lifetime if you're lucky. Then on the morning before the game I dislocated my finger and was out. It was one of the biggest disappointments I had had for a long time. Only two days before I had been commiserating with John Collins who had to pull out with a strained muscle. It's murder when you get your first game for a long time then this happens.

I was worried about missing out on my chance of playing in Italy and shouldn't have played against Hearts the following Saturday. But Chris Reid was also injured. It was a big mistake as it is probably the worst game I have played for Hibs. If I had been fit I would have saved John Robertson's free kick, and he himself said he was surprised when it went in.

It was a bad day all round for Hibs as Paul Wright was put out for the rest of the season. At first I thought he had ridden the tackle when Neil Berry lunged at him, but he stayed down. Paul was looking sharp that day and had Hearts worried. It would have been interesting to see what Paul would have done if he had played for the rest of the season. We lost seven points overall to Hearts, which was a sickener as we had been the top team the season before. It was also diabolical for the fans.

Our chance of getting a place in Europe was slipping again. After beating two top teams, Rangers and Aberdeen. We then lost 1-0 to Dundee United through a Mixu Paatalinen penalty. I though we were unlucky as against both United and Hearts we deserved at least a point in each game.

We bounced back with a 1-0 victory over Celtic thanks to a Paul Kane penalty. We thought our luck was changing as it was the first we had got in the League all season. Our old weakness returned as we slumped to the weaker clubs after more than matching the top teams. Our game against Motherwell should have been our cup final but we lost 1-0. Then in the last game of the season we still had a chance of qualifying.

Before the game we were joking in the dressing room that a penalty wouldn't go amiss. Apart from Kano's against Celtic we had only had one other against Liège in the UEFA Cup. As we bemoaned the fact we never got the breaks, some bright spark piped up that the 'reason we don't get penalties is because we never get into the box'. A slight exaggeration but there was some truth in it.

A dodgey moment. I wasn't sure what Wayne Foster wanted to do — kiss me or kill me.

Lo and behold, the gods were good to us and we got a penalty against Dundee. A dearth of them all season, then two in our run-in. We couldn't believe it, but disaster struck as John Collins missed it and our 1-1 draw meant we had missed out on Europe.

In some ways we didn't deserve it for losing so many stupid points. We had taken five off the champions Rangers and beaten Aberdeen twice yet got no joy off Hearts. Our squad had not been strengthened enough in the pre-season and injuries took their toll

D

in the run-in. Goal scoring was a big problem. Our top scorer and passport to Europe the previous season, Steve Archibald, had been allowed to leave when he could have been invaluable in the League and Europe. I had loved playing in Europe. We had lost only one goal in four games and were unlucky to go out when we did thanks to a missed penalty and a freak goal.

I felt I had to keep playing European football to improve my game. I hadn't come up here for money reasons. I wanted international and European football. Hibs could have and should have had it as we moved into the 1990-91 season. The club had potential when I arrived and for the most part I had thoroughly enjoyed my first three years. But they had wasted chances to develop the team. For a long time we knew the club was going off course. Little did we know it was heading for the rocks.

CHAPTER NINE

Grasping the Thistle

When I was a lad, my father used to kid me on that I could play for Scotland. I never took him seriously although I used to cheer on Scotland with him when we watched them on television. My first international break came with England but it was an experience that left me with a sour taste. I was selected for the Under-21s against Hungary at Portsmouth. Gary Bailey pulled out of the squad as he was injured playing for Manchester United in the cup final. I was due to play but at the last minute they brought in Alan Knight, who was then the Portsmouth keeper, to boost the crowd. I felt I had been mucked about and everyone at Oldham thought it was a disgrace. Joe Royle helped me to get over it and told me just to get on with my career as my chance would come again.

As it was, things couldn't have turned out better in the long run. Just after Alex Ferguson took over as Scotland manager Joe phoned Alex to tell him I was eligible to play for Scotland. Joe told me to expect a call from Alex Ferguson and when he called and offered me the chance it took me less than two seconds to decide. He told me I would be in the squad against East Germany and I thought he meant the Under-21 team. It was only when I joined the squad at Turnberry that I realised he meant the full team.

I travelled up with Manchester United players Gordon Strachan and Arthur Albiston who did their best to help me settle in. I was frightened to death as I didn't know how everyone would react to an English-born player who played for a Second Division club.

It was difficult at first because I wanted to prove myself and ended up diving about like a daft 'un. Alex Ferguson told me I would come on in the second half for Jim Leighton. The nerves built up and I was wondering how the crowd would react. Looking back, I now see I had nothing to worry about. At half-time Alex Ferguson told me not to strip. For a minute I thought I wasn't getting my chance until he explained I was to come on after five minutes and get a boost from the crowd. If I went out with the rest of the team no one would notice.

It was the longest five minutes of my life. I had sausages and egg for breakfast that morning and as I went on I could feel it in my throat. As Jim Leighton came off wishing me all the best, all I could say to him was 'I can still taste that sausage in my throat.'

I knew how much the Scots hate the English and was apprehensive they might look on me as an impostor. But it was unbelievable the reception I got. 50,000 Scots started singing 'Andy Goram, Andy Goram, You're not English any more.' It was unbelievable. My father cracked up in the stand and started crying. He was probably more nervous than me.

He said it was the proudest moment of his life. My father had always told me about the Scots' passion for football, and here I was experiencing the Hampden roar first hand.

I had hardly anything to do in the game except for a 20-yard shot. At least I had kept a clean sheet.

I was to get two more caps before the Scotland squad was chosen for the 1986 World Cup in Mexico. My next game was Kenny Dalglish's testimonial against Romania when I played the full game. We won 3-0 and it was a fitting tribute to one of the greatest players Scotland has ever produced. The third game I managed to keep another clean sheet when we drew 0-0 in Holland with a real mixed bag of players in a World Cup warm-up game.

I didn't want to jump to any conclusions that I would automatically be in the squad but the day Joe Royle told me after training that they had announced the squad was a real boost. I knew I was just along for the experience and only fully appreciated it when I got back.

We trained at high altitude in Santa Fe before going to Mexico. Alex Ferguson had a reputation as a really strict manager but it wasn't like a prison camp at all. It was quite relaxed and we would eat out at night and visit the local race track. We moved on to Los Angeles for a warm-up game against LA Heat before arriving in Mexico.

A few of the more senior players went out to meet Rod Stewart in Hollywood and some of them came back a wee bit worse for wear. Among them was Alan Rough and apparently Alex Ferguson had seen them. I think this was the reason why a couple of days later when the squad was announced I was named as number two keeper.

One thing that struck me was the women's game before the LA Heat match. I was taken aback by their skill. This was backed up by a recent close-season trip I took to the States. The women's game is coming on by leaps and bounds. It's way ahead of anything we have here and their women's team is among the top five in the world.

Scotland were the last team to arrive in Mexico and we were also described as the scruffiest. It had been a long journey and quite a few of the lads hadn't shaved. All the stereotypes came rolling out as Paul Sturrock was seen having a drink. The press went on about how it did not take long for the Scots to start exercising their right arms. Needless to say, Paul was having a glass of water.

Mexico itself was a nightmare. Our hotel was situated across the road from some pyramids but inside it was like a prison. There were hotel guards in every corridor and the rooms were like little caves. To make matters worse we were all in single rooms with stone walls with no wallpaper. It seemed if you had anything to say to someone you would have to tap on the pipes. Compared to our camp in Italy, it was like chalk and cheese.

We were confident for our first game against Denmark. Charlie Nicholas in particular had looked superb in training and his injury early on in the game against Denmark ruined our chances of qualifying. After Charlie was hit by a late tackle, Preben Elkjaer put Denmark ahead. Roy Aitken scored but it was ruled offside. We were dancing about on the bench when it went in and our original view was confirmed on television later on. It was a legitimate goal but the breaks were not going our way. The last thing we wanted was to start with a defeat.

Before the game a member of the press got hold of the team list and leaked it to the Danish manager Sepp Piontek. We would play four at the back, four in midfield, and one up front with another tucked in behind him. Piontek was not sure whether he should play a sweeper or not but once he was told our formation he knew what to do. Although it might not seem a big issue, it meant a lot to us. The manager had wanted to keep the team close to his chest. It was a real shock for me as I didn't realise things like that went on. How could one of our own people have helped the opposition? The 2-1 defeat against West Germany left us with everything to do against Uruguay.

We knew it wasn't a game for the meek and mild. Alex Ferguson dropped Graeme Souness who was maybe just the sort of player we needed for this type of game. Half an hour before the game I was on the pitch helping Jim Leighton warm up. The next thing we knew was there was a barrage of balls hurtling in at us. The whole of the Uruguayan team had come out and thundered down our end, belting balls everywhere. Jim and I had to duck for cover. It was like a group of kids in the park. We told them we were here first but they took no notice. There were only two of us against their whole team so we had to move up the other end. This was just the start of the intimidation.

If the Uruguayans had kept 11 men on the pitch I think we would have won. But after their captain was sent off for almost breaking Gordon Strachan's leg in the first few minutes everything went wrong. I still think the refereee pulled out the wrong card but once the red one was in the air there was no going back. From then on Uruguay dug in to defend. Enzo Francescoli had a magnificent game with the amount of work he did and almost took us on single-handed. No one can forget Steve Nicol's miss. When the ball came across, the goalie was at the near post. Stevie tried to make sure by tapping it in, but the goalie got across to save it. The Uruguayans spat at us throughout the game and Graeme Sharpe discovered a new form of intimidation. At a corner one of their defenders stuck a finger up his back passage.

You don't mind getting kicked as it's part and parcel of the game but that was a bit personal. I refused to switch shirts at the end, as did most of the lads. It was the worse behaviour any of us had come across.

I was hauled in for a drug test after the game. It was the first time for me, but there must be something about me because in six of the World Cup games I have been involved in, three times I've been selected. It happened in Italy after the Costa Rica and Brazil game. Maybe I look like a junkie or they just think I look dopey. Anyway, for Scotland it was a classic case of we were last ones in and first ones out.

I had another season at Boundary Park ahead of me before I was called up for the squad in the Rous Cup. It was a memorable week for me as my son Daniel was born and I played against Brazil.

The squad was based at Turnberry and I had been in two minds whether I should stay behind with my wife. She wanted me to go as it was a great opportunity for me. Jim Leighton had already played on the Saturday against England. We were out on the golf course when I was called in to be told my wife was in labour. Andy Roxburgh was different class about it and I went straight down to Lancashire. After Daniel was born I phoned Andy Roxburgh who congratulated me but told me I had better get back up there pronto as Jim Leighton had flu.

Every footballer dreams of playing against Brazil and the only thing that ruined it was letting in two goals. The first one I blame myself for. Valdo, who went on to become their captain in Italy, bent in what might have been a shot or a cross from the left to the near post. I scrambled across but was too late.

Although not everyone blamed me for it, I did myself. I had learned from Jim Leighton to be ultra critical of my own performance. He analysed every fault he made to see how he could improve hinself. Mirandinha had a terrific game and scored the second. Although it wasn't a full-strength Brazilian team, it was the best team I had played against.

I was always delighted to be in the squad and built up a great relationship with Jim Leighton. He and Roughie helped me when I first joined the squad and were always ready with advice. Jim had distinguished himself in Mexico and had silenced a lot of the English critics about Scottish goalkeepers.

For me it was a learning process and I realised I had to be patient. However I had to be ready to seize the chance when it came to be Scotland's number one keeper. It was to be over a year before I played again for Scotland. In the autumn after the Brazil game I moved to Hibs and for a while was out of the squad. It was good for me in the long run as I appreciated the competition and knew I mustn't take it for granted. I settled into the Premier League and my form with Hibs soon re-established me in the squad.

I returned for Scotland against Italy in Perugia, another top-class encounter. It was a World Cup warm-up for both of us and they had their young team from the European championships. To be quite honest I didn't realise how good they were and that day they gave us a bit of a lesson. It was the core of the team that played in the 1990 finals. The atmosphere in Perugia was something else. I had never experienced anything like it. Before the game I just about laid an egg when a firework exploded behind me. I thoroughly enjoyed the game as I had a lot to do. Giannini opened the scoring with a penalty which he coolly retook after the referee told him to take it again for an infringement. I noticed he was substituted before the penalty shoot-out against Argentina in the World Cup semi-finals. It is not a move I would have made as you need your top guns at such a time. Berti got the second after I parried an effort from Serena.

I had played well but knew that Jim was still the number one keeper. I would only play if he was injured. Andy Roxburgh never said I would play even when Jim came under tremendous pressure in the lead-up to the World Cup in Italy. A lot of other people, some in the press and some in football, said I would be playing but never the manager himself. Jim and I spoke about it and he had seen the same thing happen when he deputised for Alan Rough. Undoubtedly if I secured the Scotland number one slot I would have to face severe criticism if my form slumped. Through it all Jim showed great character, and the way Andy Roxburgh was loyal to him gave other players confidence. If the manager has selected you he obviously has belief in you and is prepared to stick by you.

When I got my chance again it was because Jim was injured.

This time, though, it was a bit different. So far I had only appeared in friendlies, but to get a World Cup qualifying game was another one to tell the grandchildren.

Every game I played for Scotland I felt more comfortable. I love big games and get a real charge from the atmosphere. The worst thing about playing for your country is if you let the team down you aren't just letting down a group of fans but the whole country.

The secret is to be positive and think what you can do for your country and how you will stand by your team mates. I stick to the same routine on the day of a game and as I'm superstitious, I don't like to change it.

On the big day I usually have breakfast in bed and then a light training session with Alan Hodgkinson and the other keepers. After lunch nearly everyone goes to bed, but it's something I don't do. I have seen myself as the only one playing snooker while the rest of the hotel seems deserted as everyone is asleep. We have a pre-match meal about five o'clock and not long after head off for Hampden.

The bus can be quite lively as people have different ways of showing their nerves. Some joke a lot while others are more reserved than usual. The adrenalin really starts to flow when you start to see the fans as you hit Glasgow. You get some buzz as you drive through the packed streets full of fans as you go to play for your country. We usually arrive about an hour and a quarter before the game and go straight onto the pitch as they unload the hampers with the strips. We take a stroll around to get a feel of the pitch and take note of any wind. We then come back in to get a rub down from Jim Steele. Steelie, the Celtic masseur, plays a big part in the squad. He's a nutter in the best sense of the word. His patter is non-stop and he does impersonations of his favourite characters, Tam the Tipster and the Czech coach.

By now your thoughts are channeled towards the game. Andy Roxburgh and Craig Brown go round the players geeing them up and telling you what they want from you. Then the players start winding each other up to get each other going. Tactics and the opposition have been taken care of well in advance. If we ever lose a game it isn't for lack of preparation by Andy Roxburgh. His preparation is second to none and during the week he has given us a thorough rundown on video of the opposition and what to look out for at set pieces. His knowledge of foreign players is exceptional.

I remember a newspaper article when Andy Roxburgh was appointed Scotland manager. It said what has a nice man like Andy Roxburgh done to deserve this? I think there is something in that as it must be one of the hardest jobs in football. He *is* a very nice man and quite unflappable. Craig Brown and he are a good double act. Whereas the boss is more reserved and distant from the players, Craig goes around giving us stick and telling us how we're mollycoddled staying in all these flash hotels. While Andy Roxburgh will let us have breakfast in bed, Craig Brown hates that.

Underneath, though, Andy Roxburgh is a fan who loves Scotland. He showed that in Italy but the classic case was in Cyprus. When Big Bish — Richard Gough — scored, he jumped into Bryan Gunn's arms. A risky thing to do but Bryan was on form and made his best catch all season.

As long as we didn't lose at home Andy Roxburgh felt we could qualify. The 1-1 draw against Yugoslavia was spoiled by their goal, but at least we got a point. Stojkovic struck a free kick against the post. I had gone down for it but knew it wasn't going in. I could have stretched that bit further but left it. It hit the outside edge of the post and cannoned off about 40 yards away. I'd like to think I could tip shots away with such force so I was taken aback when the referee gave a corner. As the corner came over someone missed it and the ball bobbed around a ruck of players before Katanec hit it in off Paul McStay's thigh. We could have done with two points, but at least we hadn't lost.

Beating Norway in Oslo had got us off to a great start and was our most important result as it gave us a great advantage. Two points away from home in our first match. The French game at Hampden, though, was the best atmosphere of any game I had ever been at. Maurice Johnston was magnificent that night and we had beaten the team who were the original favourites in the group. The great escape in Cyprus was another all-important result. Big Roy Aitken spurred Scotland on to victory that day and few will forget the scenes on the bench when Richard Gough scored the winner in injury time. Andy Roxburgh had the substitutes on the go all the time in the second half. It was only later he revealed they were on the track to act as ball boys to stop Cyprus time wasting.

In the French game Jim Leighton silenced a lot of his critics with a fine performance but the result in Yugoslavia and Paris stirred it up again. Manchester United's poor league form didn't help matters either. Every time Jim made a mistake it seemed to be on television. Of course I was desperate to get into the team but I wanted to do it on my own efforts, not on the back of a merciless campaign against Jim Leighton. I had roomed with Jim for five years with Scotland and we had been through a lot together. I had also learnt a hell of a lot from him. Some of the criticism he was getting was diabolical. Former professionals who should have known better were joining in and some of Jimmy Greaves' criticism on television was unbelievable. I sometimes think Jimmy built his TV reputation by having a go at Scottish keepers. One thing I can tell you is he knows nothing about goalkeeping.

When Jim Leighton was dropped before the English cup final replay, Bryan Gunn and myself phoned him. We were with the Scotland squad for the friendly against Egypt when we heard the news. We realised what a blow it would be to him and he was quite distraught. There isn't much you can really say in a situation like that, but it shows the good relationship there was amongst the three of us.

Obviously Jim's confidence had taken a bad knock, but the World Cup was the best thing that could have happened. Instead of brooding all summer over being dropped from the cup final, he came out to join the squad in Malta.

Bryan Gunn and myself hated seeing Jim getting slaughtered in the press and we made a pact to watch what we said as we knew people were trying to stir it up amongst us. One paper offered me a four-figure sum to stick the knife into Jim but I turned it down. There was no way I could turn on him.

Criticism is part and parcel of the professional game. You get heaps of praise when you do well but you know there will come a day when the boot goes in. If you don't accept that, you're as well chucking it. Instead I'm intent on delaying that day as long as possible. Also you have to learn to live with disappointments. In the run-up to the finals I had been due to play against Argentina. It was a vital match for me as I could stake a further claim for the Scotland job. As we were winding up our final training session on the morning of the game, Roy Aitken had one last shot. As I dived for the ball it knicked the top of my finger. I knew straight away it was dislocated but thought if it's put back in it should be alright. However it ballooned up and I had to pull out. I was really disappointed but before the game I was doing a radio interview and the reporter was saying just that to me. Behind him were a few people in wheelchairs and I told him yes, I was disappointed, but seeing these people there put it all in perspective. I had a great life as a professional footballer and was luckier than a lot of people. You also realise that about being in the squad. Although you may not get a game, at least you're there. Many other players would love to be in your shoes.

My chance came again in warm-up games against East Germany, Malta and Poland. In the build-up to Italy so many people kept telling me I would be playing, but I was taking nothing for granted. Until Andy Roxburgh gave me the nod I wouldn't believe it.

After starting the qualifying group so well, Scotland's form had floundered. The defeats in France and Yugoslavia had hit us hard and the final game against Norway was nerve-wracking. Erland Johnsen's 40-yard shot caught Jim Leighton out and we had to sweat a bit in the final minutes. After the game the celebrations were fairly muted. I had been expecting a champagne party but there was just a general sense of relief.

We continued to gift goals in the warm-up games. I felt sorry for Bryan Gunn against Egypt. It was a good chance for him but the team had a stinker. Whenever that happens, it's likely the keeper is going to get some stick. Too many of the players were jaded from the Aberdeen-Celtic cup final and you hardly expect a 40-yard pass back like Gordon Durie's in a game like that. Of course that led to the first goal.

In the other three games we scored two own goals and gave away a penalty. In Malta I was at fault with the goal. A cross came over and I started to come for it but realised I wouldn't make it. As I started to go back to my line I slipped. Meanwhile Craig Levein had missed it and the ball struck Dave McPherson's knee and bounced in. The press shared the blame around, but I felt I could have done better.

I had less of a chance in the game against Poland at Hampden. As a long ball came through I thought Gary Gillespie was going to head it back to me. He let it bounce so I came off my line for the pass back. Next thing I knew it was whistling past me into the back of the net. I'm sure if Gary had been fully fit he wouldn't have made the mistake and probably couldn't do it again even if he tried. However, it was a serious problem for us. You cannot afford to give away ridiculous goals at the top level. We had done it in the qualifiers and now we were doing it in the warm-ups. We headed off to Italy under a cloud. Too many people forgot what a good job Andy Roxburgh had done in getting us there, but now was our chance to redeem ourselves.

The Scotland squad had travelled to Rapallo in February to familiarise ourselves with Italy. It was a perfect camp and in a different class compared to Mexico. The local team had spent £100,000 returfing their pitch for us to train on. We felt we had a better chance than ever before of qualifying for the second round. Also we should be able to get an all-important win in our first game against Costa Rica.

Everything went well at training although Jim Leighton and I never discussed who would be playing. Two days before the game Andy Roxburgh saw the squad in separate groups to tell us who would be playing. He had the goalkeepers in first. Jim, Bryan and myself went in to meet Andy Roxburgh, Craig Brown, Tommy Craig and Alan Hodgkinson. I had always thought Jim would be playing despite what everyone else said. The manager had stuck by him through thick and thin in the past. At the team meetings in Rapallo, whenever he was talking about a situation involving the goalkeepers, he would look at Jim as though giving an indication to him that he would be playing. That got to me a bit.

We both knew that whoever played would get 100 per cent back-up from the other. As we all sat down Andy said this was no time for sentimental chit chat and came straight out with it. 'Jim's

playing because of his experience.' He then went on to explain
how Scotland would be playing.

I had been hit by a bombshell. These were the dreaded words I
didn't want to hear. My heart sank and my eyes glazed over. I
never heard a word Andy Roxburgh said after that. It was just
one of those situations when you drift off into space somewhere.
When the meeting was over we got up to go. On the way out the
door Jim reached over to shake my hand and said he was sorry I
wouldn't be getting a game. If I had been picked, I would have
done the same.

I was walking about in a daze and went up to my room. After a
while I phoned my local pub in Bonnyrigg, The Calderwood, I
wanted something to cheer me up and had a laugh with one of the
lads, 'Rocket' Ronnie Pinkman.

I was surprised how much it had affected me. I had been
preparing myself for it but it still devastated me. I then phoned my
wife and spoke to my son Daniel. That helped me as well. It's hard
to explain how I felt but it was the worst feeling I had had in
football. I can't even remember the next training session as I was
still in space somewhere.

All the thoughts I had had looking forward to a chance to play
in the World Cup evaporated with these six words: 'Jim's playing
because of his experience.'

But I realised I had another job to do now. I had to help Jim
prepare for the game. Jim and I began to speak about it and I told
him all along I thought he would play. Jim said, to be honest, he
thought so too by the way Andy Roxburgh had been looking at
him during the meetings.

Some of the press tried to get me to hit out about it but we stuck
to our pact of keeping all comments to a minimum. Jim in
particular was giving them a wide berth after all he had had to
take from them in the last few months.

At the worst we thought we'd get a point off Costa Rica. Little
did we know it was going to go down as one of the black days in
Scottish football history. Costa Rica's get-out was their wide men.
Whenever they were in trouble they pushed it out to the wings.
Scotland, though, played with four midfield players who were all
central midfield men. So the two wide men tended to un-
consciously drift into the middle.

We had 19 attempts at goal and 17 corners. They only had three attempts at goal. That just about sums it up. Before the game their keeper Conejo had been identified as weak on crosses but he had a brilliant game. Costa Rica were also very well coached. At one stage their manager Bora Milutinovic appeared at the touchline when someone was injured with a pen and paper. He called over a couple of players and drew a tactical instruction. They were a better team than most of us thought but still there are no excuses. We should have won.

Just as in Mexico, we had lost the first game. Now we had everything to play for against Sweden. In between, though, we had one of those little escapades that tend to be a feature with Scotland during the World Cup. Mo Johnston and Jim Bett were splashed all over the papers supposedly out on a bender the day after the Costa Rica game. The whole thing was blown out of all proportion and they hadn't broken any curfew or drink ban. How could they when there wasn't one in the first place? The players had been allowed to go into town for a meal and a few drinks and the photographer who spotted Mo was about a hundred yards away. He was sniping at him and Jim Bett through a telephoto lens. Mo has the reputation that unless he's spotted in church he must be up to no good. But even if the players didn't misbehave, that wasn't going to stop sections of the press providing some scandal anyway.

The shame of it all was that Andy Roxburgh didn't treat us like kids, and we weren't going to let him down.

He also made sure we weren't bored. One evening he called us to a meeting at nine o'clock. Most of us were not that keen as the boss is quite partial to his meetings. We all assembled anyway and Andy said we could have a few beers. All of a sudden he starts passing out song sheets. I thought what's this, are we going to start singing hymns? Ally McCoist stood up with a microphone and announced tonight we had some top-class acts about to perform for us. We didn't realise it was ourselves. Everybody had to get up and do a turn. Gary Gillespie was the star of the show closely followed by Alan McInally singing 'Streets of London' and Ally McCoist doing his Bruce Springsteen impersonation. The goalies did a pretty awful version of 'My Way' while Gary Gillespie finished the night off leading us into 'You'll Never Walk Alone'. He had to stop during it as he got a bit emotional, but we all carried on. It was a superb evening and there was hardly a dry eye in the house. Bryan Gunn was the worst singer of the lot and the management did their bit as well, although Craig Brown was nowhere to be seen. We knew it was a special night as Hughie Allan almost smiled on one occasion.

As we went in against Sweden we knew it was do or die. Going to the game, as I looked at the fans I thought without a doubt they must be the best in the world. One scene that stuck out was a Scots guy belting along on a scooter beside our bus with a Swede on the back. The Scottish fans were superb that night and it was the most emotional atmosphere in a dressing room since I had been in the squad. It was unbelievable how wound up we all were. We were shouting and screaming at each other how we were going to beat the other lot. When we lined up in the tunnel Glenn Hysen was at the front looking cool as ever. He knew Gary Gillespie and some of the other Anglos. But the rest of their team looked like the nice boy next door. Not one of them looked a real hard nut. They were all pleasant chaps and none of them would put the fear of God into you.

I took a look along our line and you couldn't get a bigger contrast. Roy Aitken, at the front, smeared with vaseline on his forehead looked as if he was about to climb in beside Mike Tyson. Jim Leighton behind him is not exactly noted for his looks. Then there was Alex McLeish who would give himself a fright in the mirror.

Big Roy had obviously been weighing all this up. He turned round to us and says, 'These guys are all shitting themselves. Look at them!'

I took a look at the Swedes and their eyes were all glazed. Big Roy starts shouting, 'Let's get into these Swedish bastards'. The whole line of us joined in shouting and screaming at the Swedes. It was as though someone had let us out of our cages. I swear the Swedes bottled it there and then in the tunnel. I looked across at Thomas Ravelli, the Swedish keeper, and his eyes were just about popping out of his head.

The rest of us took our place on the bench still growling as the teams kicked off. Within a minute the ball came loose right in the middle of the park, and about ten tackles went in. Once the ball moved on where there were still blue shirts flying in. The attitude of the Scots that night summed up for me what the Scots are all about.

When Stuart McCall, one of the surprise packages of the team, scored we knew they were finished. At half-time when I was warming up on the pitch with Ally McCoist the crowd were going berserk. I spotted this girl on a barrier waving like mad. I thought she was waving as if she knew me but I didn't know any girls who were over for the game. I turned to Coistie and says, 'What about her there? She's going daft.' He just shrugs and tells me, 'Oh aye, it's my girl.' I couldn't believe it. There she was going mental in the crowd with all the rest of the punters. The Scots are definitely a breed apart.

In the second half on the bench Ally McCoist and Alan McInally, two of the biggest mental cases in the squad, were holding up empty plastic bottles, singing all the songs with the fans. When the Mexican wave came around the ground the bench joined in with them. We really went crazy when the penalty was awarded. As big Roy broke free and went past the goalie I never thought it was a penalty. The big man's one of the fliest guys around and went down in a heap.

Maurice Johnston cooly scored and we knew we had a chance of qualifying on two points, but that was leaving our fate in other people's hands.

After a couple of beers that night we went to bed knackered. We were all drained and had used up so much adrenalin at the game.

Getting a point against Brazil was now easier said than done. We had moved camps to Saint Vincent in the foothills of the Alps near Turin. The biggest thing we had to do against Brazil was conquer the shirts. If you put them in a different strip they aren't the same. However, for 80 minutes we held them in the superb Stadio di Alpi. The rain that night suited us and it was almost like playing in Scotland. Halfway through the second half the Brazilians seemed to have settled for a draw. They were quite happy with that and the news that Costa Rica were beating Sweden lifted us all.

The only moment of concern came when Murdo McLeod was hit on the head at a free kick. Just before it was taken Ally McCoist, fly as ever, switched places with Murdo. Coistie didn't want to ruin his good looks, whereas Murdo had none anyway.

Just when everything seemed to be going our way we lost a goal. Because Jim Leighton was playing so well there was only Gary Gillespie following up when Careca shot. On the greasy surface he failed to hold it and it spun clear straight to Muller. If Jim had been playing badly there probably would have been two or three defenders in the box who could have cleared. As we pushed for an equaliser their keeper Taffarel made the save of the tournament, as far as I'm concerned, from a Mo Johnston shot.

Once again Scotland had failed to qualify. Going back in the plane with Jim Leighton, we compared Italy to Mexico. The '86 squad had been stronger with players like Souness, Strachan and Miller and McLeish at their prime. This squad had come closer than any other team to qualifying. We had done well in the qualifying round and with a bit of luck could have got to the second stage of the finals.

Some of the lads were glad to be going home but that was an attitude I couldn't understand. It was my second World Cup and I relished every minute of it. There were some great memories and it was very well organised by the Italians. However, it was the poorest standard of a World Cup I can remember and the refereeing was a disgrace. But to be there is the pinnacle of the game for every professional.

Now I want to make it third time lucky and go with Scotland to America in 1994. Only this time I hope I'm playing. I don't understand why any player doesn't want to be part of the international team. It is the ultimate peak of our profession. I love being in the squad and my ambition is to establish myself as Scotland's first choice keeper. Once I'm in there you'll have a hard job getting me out.

CHAPTER TEN

Living in the Limelight

Some people seek controversy and others it seems to follow around. I suppose I fall into the second category. One thing I would like to make clear to Hibs fans is that I have never gone looking for trouble with the club and every game I have played I have been totally committed.

I have had a great time at Hibs and my only regret is we lost a great opportunity to put the club back up where it belongs. After the takeover trouble we're back to square one. It will now be a hard struggle for Hibs in the coming seasons but I'm sure they will be back as one of Scotland's top clubs.

It irritates me when people question my commitment to Hibs. All professional footballers know they're on a conveyor belt, and it's more a feature of the game today than it ever was. The days of the one-club player seem to be a thing of the past. But I want to put on record that I asked Hibs for a five-year contract in March 1990 and they turned it down. The money was not the problem. They would only offer me an extra year to my present contract. I refused to sign as a tax problem arose over the signing-on fee. At the time I had also put in offers for two houses, and if either had been accepted I would probably have signed.

But the fact that Hibs would not give me a five-year contract summed up for me the lack of interest in the club at the time about what was happening on the pitch. Obviously those pulling the financial strings were more interested in the stock exchange and what was happening in the south of England property market.

Jim Gray later told me when we were thrashing out my position at the end of the season that he couldn't trust me for a five-year contract because of the way I lived. What that meant I don't know. I think he has some fancy idea I'm some sort of high-rolling champagne charlie.

It's an image I'm fed up with. Just because you go to the pub and have a few drinks, you get branded an alcoholic. Just because you like a bet at the bookies, rumours spread that you owe thousands.

My reputation has been blown out of all proportion because Edinburgh's a wee village. When I first came here I thought it was a big city but I was amazed when people would say 'I heard you were at such and such a place the other night.' I have a reputation as a bit of a lad because I get on well with the fans and am seen to socialise with them. But I'm no different from any punter, so I don't see why I can't go out with the boys, and have a few drinks and a laugh. All of a sudden because I play for Hibs I'm not allowed to do that. I know I have a responsibility to the club and my country, but I don't think I have ever let either of them down.

Some of the stories about my gambling are incredible. One newspaper approached me saying they had a story that I owed a major bookie £40,000. I laughed in the reporter's face and told him to go ahead and print it. I would enjoy making a few quid from sueing them for printing such nonsense.

These stories are outrageous. It's no secret that I enjoy a bet and I have never tried to deny it. I may owe money for a couple of weeks but I always pay it back. I would challenge anybody to say I owe ridiculous amounts and I resent the fact it gets bandied about. I have no intention of changing my lifestyle. Why should I? I have played for Scotland at both football and cricket doing what I do. If someone will give me a good reason I'll consider it.

One thing I do resent is that these rumours led to a major club pulling out when it looked as if they were going to make a move for me.

Despite all that, my interest in the turf is not just confined to a bookies shop. For over a year now I have had part share in a racehorse. My mare Pollybrig is trained by Ken Oliver down in the Borders. It is something I have always fancied doing, and since coming to play for Hibs the opportunity has arisen.

The real VIPs — the fans. I always have time for them. After all where would the game be without them.

One of the best moves I made was leaving the city for a while to live in Bonnyrigg. I left Edinburgh because my car was sprayed and damaged on a few occasions. You also have to take a lot of stick and abuse when you go out on the town. I was fed up with the hassle, and Gordon Rae told me there was a house going near him in Bonnyrigg, so I moved there.

Bonnyrigg is a former mining community and the people are top class and treated me as one of them. I had a great local, The Calderwood, where I regularly played pool and cards. They're a terrific bunch who kidded me on like anyone else and treated me as one of the lads, not Andy Goram the footballer.

When I look back on it I don't think Hibs had the money to offer me a five-year contract. At the time Jim Gray said it was a fallacy to say Hibs didn't have the money to pay me. Well, I think events since then have proved my point. It needed Wallace Mercer's outrageous attempt to take over Hibs to really expose what was happening at the club. In the long run it will be better for Hibs that the board was changed, but it is tragic to think they got into that position in the first place.

Hibs have some of the prettiest fans.

Although I have had my fall-outs with manager Alex Miller, my relationship with the football staff has been very good. Alex Miller is an underrated manager. He has an excellent knowledge of the game, and the fact that he was one of Scotland's coaches in Italy shows how he is regarded by people in the game. A lot of people may say he is a dour, defensive manager, but there is a lighter side to his character. It should also be appreciated that he has been limited with the players he has had to work with. Likewise it isn't as if he has had an open cheque book.

So many managers like to hog the limelight and take the praise when things go well. Alex Miller, though, always redirects it towards the players. But he's a real bawler and is very critical in the dressing room. Partly this is because he is obsessed with the technical side of the game and is an absolute perfectionist. This is probably why he's always getting on at us. To him a match is like a chess game and you can see he's always trying to outwit the other manager.

While Joe Royle at Oldham liked to keep in close contact with

Catch 'em young.

the players and was worried about getting cut off from them, Alex Miller is the opposite. He maintains a barrier between the players and management, but on the occasions he does loosen up a bit he's very good company.

One of the biggest surprises since I have been at Hibs was when Peter Cormack left. You could never split up Alex Miller and Peter. They were always together at training or even on the bus to games. The first real wind we got that something was wrong was when they started sitting apart from each other on the bus to away games about a month before the end of the season. We all immediately noticed it, and as it got more obvious there was open speculation about a fall-out.

I was at a World Cup dinner on the night before Peter left the

A future rival for my job?

club, but he never mentioned anything about it. You could tell Peter didn't want to be an assistant forever. He had been a manager before and had played at the top level with Liverpool. He had his own ideas on the game and when the boss went into hospital with a gallstone he rearranged the training. He was like a kid let loose with the run of the place.

On the Monday before the last game of the season Alex Miller walked into the dressing room and told us Peter had parted company with the club. He added, 'I'm the manager who makes

The perks of the job. Ian McDonald presents me with the keys for my sponsored car.

the decisions and that's it.' We then went and started training. We all had our whispers about what had happened, but the timing of it struck me as strange. We only had one game to go and still had a chance of qualifying for Europe. A lot of the boys were sorry to see Peter go but, as I've said, this is one of the basic facts about football.

I must admit I have given the boss his fair share of headaches in my time. I don't try to be a rebel, but I will stick to my guns when I think I am in the right, as with the cricket dispute. However, there are times when I am not. Some fans may remember when we played Celtic in the cup in February 1988. The game was televised live on a Sunday afternoon and everyone could see I was sporting a real keeker of a black eye. I got some stick from the lads as Archie McPherson described it as the result of an accident in training. Well, it didn't happen like that. On the Thursday night before the game I had been at a 'Question of Sport' do in Glasgow, and after it I had gone for a drink at The Savoy with some of the other players. We were relaxing having a drink when a few words were exchanged between the company I was with and another group.

The next thing I knew this character came flying over and I went to stop him. The pair of us ended up rolling about on the floor and that is where I picked up my black eye. As we were split up, Ally McCoist did the best thing and led me out of the hotel.

Next morning I walked into training with a real shiner. The boss took one look and automatically I came out with the old walking-into-a-door routine. Of course, that went down like a lead balloon so I had to come clean. I told him that somebody had said the chap in question was a croupier who knew Alex Miller. The boss said he didn't know any croupiers, but when I mentioned his name, Billy Jones, he said he had heard of him. The gentleman in question had a bit of a reputation in Glasgow, and it wasn't for flower arranging. Alex Miller told me just to forget about it, but no sooner said than done he got a phone call from the guy. He was known around Rangers circles and the boss knew who he was from his playing days. Now he was asking if he could come through and use the gym at Easter Road. The boss told him, 'Billy, you're a big lad. You don't need any building up.' The guy explained, 'It's just so I can sort your goalie out. I heard he wanted to see me.'

I can tell you nothing was further from the truth, especially after what I had heard about him. Thankfully the boss sorted the situation out and then promptly fined me for being out two days before a game. The whole incident taught me a lesson and I was just pleased to put it all behind me.

Since then I have met the guy a few times when I have been through in Glasgow with the Scotland squad. I am pleased to say we had a joke about it and I would like to think we get on quite well now. I am also sorry that I had to get Alex Miller involved in the whole affair.

Football management must be one of the hardest jobs around. Your fate is in other people's hands more than in most jobs. At least as a player you know you can still play in a poor team but if your own performance is good, people will notice it. When I finish playing I think I will give management a body swerve. I want to enjoy life, not get an ulcer. One thing that does appeal to me is

I never knew Mickey Weir could read. Here he studies my autograph to see how it's done.

coaching goalkeepers. Alan Hodgkinson set a precedent when he started doing it.

Probably when I retire there will be so many doing it there won't be the same opportunities. But the game is changing fast. I don't think a lot of people in Scotland realise how much at times. In the summer of 1990 I went over to do some coaching in America with Peter Bonetti in Boston. It was a marvellous opportunity and opened my eyes to a few things.

I had been told the school ran from nine to eleven o'clock daily. So I thought I was in for an easy time. It wasn't that different from training here. However, I was in for a big surprise. The course lasted from nine in the morning till eleven at night. I was knackered after the first couple of days and lost half a stone in a week.

The approach of the American kids and adults could teach people here a lot of things. The oldest on the course was a 30-year-old woman and we had both the American and Canadian women's teams' keepers. The US women's keeper was as good as some of the keepers I have seen in the lower leagues in England. People over here might find that hard to take but I'm telling you it's true. I was surprised at the number of women playing the game.

The Americans' attitude was something else. They threw themselves about on brick-hard ground and cuts, grazes, staved fingers didn't dampen their enthusiasm one iota.

They got three sessions a day and still some of them would be asking for more. If you had told them to run into a tree they would have done it.

The attitude of many professionals here is as soon as the boss says that's it at training they can't get off quick enough to get home. But the Americans have no half-measures. If they're going to do something they will do it properly and are always ready to keep learning.

I like to believe I have the same attitude. I am always looking to learn. Alan Hodgkinson has been my guru. He has taught me so much. All along the way I have picked up tips from other keepers. When Peter McCloy came to do some training at Hibs, I learned from him. Coaching with Peter Bonetti last summer, I picked up a tip about your stance as you go for crosses. Tony Meola, the US World Cup keeper, came on the course and told me how he had added six inches to his vertical jump in six months by doing power exercises on his legs. He could also jump across the 18-yard box in five strides. I could only manage it in five and a half. All these little things add up.

Going to the World Cup gave me the chance to study the world's best keepers. Taffarel of Brazil stood out, but maybe it was because their goalkeepers don't tend to be their strong point. Zenga of Italy was class but I would like to see how he would do if he didn't have such a superb defence in front of him. Conejo of Costa Rica was brilliant against Scotland and Higuita of Colombia was top-class entertainment. Goycochea of Argentina got lucky, and one to watch in England with Queens Park Rangers is Stejskal of Czechoslovakia.

The two recent experiences at the World Cup and in America taught me how fast football is developing and how you cannot afford to get left behind. You must always have an open mind and cannot remain parochial. New ideas and new methods must be welcomed both by the professionals and administrators in the Scottish game.

So far the game has been good to me. I have learned a lot and intend to keep on doing so. I still have many ambitions, but one thing looms above all others. That is to establish myself as Scotland's number one goalkeeper.

CHAPTER ELEVEN

Making it on Merit

I approached the start of the 1990-91 season under a bit of a cloud. I was still uncertain about my future with Hibs and must admit my experience at the World Cup had got to me. Not only was I not sure where my future lay, there was an air of uncertainty around Easter Road. Many pundits had written the club off after the takeover débâcle and were predicting Hibs were doomed to relegation. The precarious state Hibs had gotten into had been exposed for everyone to see. The big question now was how would the club get over it? Wallace Mercer had brought out a video the previous Christmas called 'Back from the Brink'. Dramatic stuff indeed! But what he had done over the last decade was small potatoes compared to what Hibs were faced with now. The situation would be a real test of the club and the people running it.

In many ways I had been cut off from the situation because the takeover bid broke just as I was about to leave with the Scotland squad for Italy. At first I thought it was a massive wind-up. When I looked at the paper I checked the date to see if it was April 1st. But it soon became evident the whole thing was in deadly earnest. I couldn't understand how they would get away with it.

You cannot just disband a club that has existed for over a century. Hibs may not have the biggest support in Scotland but the fans are just as passionate as Hearts fans, if not more so. Also what struck me was what would happen to the players. It was alright for me as I knew my place would be secure, but what about the young lads at the club? Were they just to be thrown on the scrap heap before they had really started out on their careers?

Hearts players, as well, would be under threat. The whole management structure would be changed and there was speculation that both sets of backroom staff, not just Hibs', would get sacked.

As I have said already, in many ways it was a blessing in disguise. We had all had our suspicions that Hibs were in trouble, but never realised to what extent. At least everything was now brought into the open and people who really cared for the club could help get things back in order. The only problem was it was Wallace Mercer who was the catalyst that set everything in motion. He was the wrong person to do it.

Wallace Mercer is Wallace Mercer. That is all I have to say. Everybody has their own opinions about him and I cannot add anything to what has been said already. Credit, though, where credit is due. He has done the business at Tynecastle. However, I have often wondered, if he has all the money and backing he says he has, why does he not just put it into Hearts? Why bother getting involved with Hibs? I am sure that must have occurred to a lot of Hearts fans as well. I also think there was somebody else behind it all. Let me put it this way — we all have our own ideas who that was. But it was confusing for the players who were in Italy. We had to concentrate on the World Cup. I spoke to the Hearts players about it and they thought it was a crazy idea. We never thought it could really happen. Dave McPherson and I joked about having a fight to see who would be captain.

The players knew that whatever happened we were just pawns who would get shuffled around. It was the punters I really felt for. They have been Hibbies a lot longer than me. We players move on in life on the 'conveyor belt' but, year in year out, it's the fans who keep the club going. You had to be around to experience the passion they put into saving the club as was seen at the 'Hands Off Hibs' rallies at Easter Road and the Usher Hall. These were very emotional occasions and the fans showed what they were made of when they were needed. Also everyone appreciated how many Hearts fans gave Hibs their support.

Back in Italy I was a bit insecure, not knowing whether I would be sold or not. I saw Jim Gray and David Duff when they came out to see the Sweden game and they were adamant the takeover would not go ahead. You have to give them credit as they fought it out. There was no point in recriminations at this stage and I think they came through for the club. They told me that David Rowland had asked them down to London as he thought it was the right time to sell his shares and he had a buyer. At first they thought it was Robert Maxwell. Rowland then told them the buyer was here waiting to meet them and in walked Wallace Mercer. You can imagine the shock they got. I would have given a £1,000 to see their faces at that moment.

But all that is history now as the takeover bid was booted into touch. Tom Farmer had come along and helped save the club, and Alister Dow was brought in to sort out the mess the plc was in.

I was only back for a few days from Italy when I had to go to America for a coaching school. Meanwhile there was a lot of press speculation that I was going to be sold. At that time I intended to leave Hibs as I didn't feel I was getting paid what I deserved. Six months before, negotiations had broken down over a new contract. I had wanted a five-year contract, which was adding three years onto the two I still had to go. At the time Hibs had knocked that back, and now I know they didn't have the money.

But all along I had told Jim Gray I would sign tomorrow if they could offer me the terms I wanted. Goalkeepers do not get sold as regularly as other players, so I knew that my next contract, whether it was with Hibs or somebody else, had to be a good one. Manchester City had been interested at the end of the previous season but hadn't offered what Hibs were wanting. Then my old club Oldham came in with the best offer to date of £1.25 million. I would have gone, and I went as far as asking Andy Roxburgh if it would affect my Scotland place. He told me it would not go against me as the second division is a hard league to play in. I looked on it as another challenge and this season would be probably Oldham's best chance of getting promotion. They had just had a great season and I have already said how highly I think of Joe Royle. I had a lot of happy memories of Oldham and was ready to go.

Hibs again knocked back Oldham's bid. Here they were valuing me at £1.5 million, yet I was only getting paid as a £300,000 player. I wondered how the club could balance that out. I was still on the £350-a-week wage I was getting when I first signed for Hibs. A lot of people are probably surprised at that. Not all footballers are as highly paid as you read in the press. But you only hear about the big contracts players are getting. Still I was bitter that Hibs were denying me the chance to go and make some money for myself.

I couldn't speak to Jim Gray at times, as we were in a continual state of conflict. I was either wanting to leave or get a new contract, while they were wanting to tie me down on terms I didn't want. However, since I have signed back on for Hibs, relations have been very good between us. It may seem funny, but that's how things go in football. I know I am not the first one to go through this sort of thing and won't be the last.

But still, at that time I was very unsettled. Hibs were due to go on their pre-season tour to Germany and I missed the plane. I wasn't trying to stage some sort of a rebellion. I was just so disappointed at not getting a move that I wasn't in the right frame of mind to go. I know if I had gone I would have let not just myself down, but the team as well. Of course, it made the news and got taken out of context. I hadn't gone AWOL as was reported, but stayed at home for three days. I was actually ill for a couple of days and couldn't eat. But nobody bothered to find out about that.

I teamed up with the squad again when they returned and went down south for a few games. I was fined by the club for not going to Germany, which I thought was a bit harsh. However, I could see their point of view and I just accepted it. Once I got back into pre-season training I began to feel a lot better and really enjoyed it. Now I had set my mind on seeing my contract out until October 1991. Then I would go abroad. Hibs had cost me a lot of money by not letting me go or giving me a new contract. So now they would have to miss out on a big transfer fee when my contract ran out. I felt really bitter about it. I was sure there weren't many players who were internationalists and valued at £1.5 million yet were getting only £350 a week.

After four games into the season we were bottom of the league

With fiancée Tracy.

with only one point. This only made me more intent than ever on seeing my contract out. The last time I tried to sort out a contract it had dragged on for months. Now I was going to keep my head down and just concentrate on playing. There was no way I was going to let my form suffer both because of my professional pride and because I owed it to the fans.

It was at this time that Bert Brown and Royal Life came into the picture. I knew Bert as a friend and he is the cousin of my fiancée Tracy. He has been Hibs daft all his life and I knew that he had wanted to do something for the club for quite a while.

Out of the blue I got a phone call to come in and see Jim Gray on a Thursday night at Easter Road. So I went in and one hour later walked out with a new three-year contract. It had taken three months the last time and then everything had collapsed. This time I was being offered a better contract than I was originally after. Royal Life had put in the money to help finance the contract Hibs were offering. I had no hesitation in accepting the deal. It gave me the chance to settle down with Tracy in Edinburgh and gave me a bit of financial security.

So with business completed Jim Gray, Bert Brown, Tracy and myself went for a curry at The Raj in Leith and celebrated. The deal suited everybody — Hibs, Royal Life, and me of course.

Jim Gray was great about it all. I had said all along I would sign, and now Hibs were offering me everything I wanted. I had also told Jim Gray there was no point in me signing on for three years if the club was not going to sign more new players. We would end up down the swannie again if nothing happened. He assured me Hibs had plans and this time they would make sure they didn't go off course like the last time. Hibs, he assured me, were not in as bad a state as people thought. He also promised there would be an internationalist at the club within two weeks.

It took a bit longer than two weeks, but, true to Jim Gray's word, Murdo McLeod arrived at Easter Road. This has been a terrific boost to the club as Murdo is just the sort of player we needed.

He had come to see the team when they were over in Germany for pre-season training, but I believe the first approach was made when he was back over for the Romania game. Alex Miller approached him, but kept it very low key. Hibs had lost out before when news of our interest in a player such as Darren Jackson had got out. The only two signings they have managed to keep under wraps were me and Murdo.

However, Dunfermline joined Hibs in an effort to get him, but it says a lot for Murdo and Hibs that he joined us although they had offered £50,000 more. I know a lot of players who would have walked to Dunfermline for that extra £50,000.

If Murdo had turned us down it would have been a real kick in the teeth for Hibs. No disrespect to Dunfermline, but they are a smaller club than Hibs. It was a real boost that a player of Murdo's standing and experience had faith in Hibs' future.

Murdo is a very popular player and he can pass on so much to the younger players. Hibs not only have a lot of potential in the first-team squad, but there are some very good 15 and 16-year-olds with the club. These boys will look up to Murdo and see what it takes to get to the very top of your profession.

I didn't know Murdo was the internationalist Jim Gray was talking about but I had an idea. All the English-based players were on contracts so it would have to be a foreign-based player and I figured out Murdo might be wanting to return to Scotland. I was delighted Hibs had kept their promise they gave me when I had signed my contract. It also shut up a lot of Jim Gray's critics who had been trying to shoot him and the club down. I have had my fall-outs with Jim Gray in the past, and who's to say it won't happen again? It's part of his job that he is on the rough edge when it comes to dealing with contracts. There are bound to be disagreements.

However, Hibs have given me a great deal and it gave me the chance to settle down in Edinburgh, which is what I wanted.

Murdo McLeod's signing has been a plus in every way and he is definitely somebody I would rather play with than against. He will add a lot of bite to our midfield and is an out-and-out winner. As well as that he is a great talker which, as I've said, is something that has been lacking at Hibs since I have been at the club.

A lot of people thought we would miss John Collins but I don't think we have missed him at all. We have missed Steve Archibald more than John Collins. This isn't being critical of John as he's a great player. He did his bit for Hibs and looks like he will do the business at Celtic. If I went, people would say the team would miss me but someone else would come in. Aberdeen never missed Jim Leighton when he left although everybody thought they would. Along came Theo Snelders and that was that. Apart from players coming and going I thought it was important that Alex Miller signed a new contract. Many people, right up to the last minute, were predicting he would go and I know there were many fans who were not pleased when he got a new contract. I know I'm repeating myself, but what do they want? He is the most successful manager at the club for over a decade, yet he still gets stick. If everybody at the club worked as hard as the boss, we would have no problems.

He has had to take the team through a very difficult patch and everyone realises we have to stick in to survive. The best results we have had this season have been when we have fought, kicked and scratched for a result. When we have gone out and got a bit cocky, trying to play a bit, we have lost. The boss has been driving this into us and we have been back in for training on Monday and Tuesday afternoons. We have to get rid of the mentality whereby you rely on two or three players. Everyone has to do their bit.

Another problem was injuries at the beginning of the season, but our midfield will stiffen up with Brian Hamilton back after his leg break. He is someone else the fans should learn to appreciate. Paul Wright is also getting sharper all the time after his injury.

It says a lot for the manager and the character of the team the way we have kept going despite what happened in the summer and getting only one point in our first four games. It's funny how fans can be, though. Against Meadowbank in the League Cup they were booing us off after 90 minutes but we still had another 30 minutes to play. That doesn't help. Yet when we were at Pittodrie for the first league game they were terrific although we lost. We deserved the stick we got from them against Raith as we were rubbish. But Raith have proved since then that they are no mugs.

But I wonder if the fans realise what an effect they can have. Celtic's fans win so many points for the club by the way they get right behind the team till the final whistle, and even after it. Hibs fans are superb away from home, but very critical at Easter Road. Maybe it's because there is such a tradition of good football at Easter Road they expect a lot. But because Hibs are not one of the most fashionable clubs at the moment, I think people underestimate the support. When we played Dundee United at Tannadice they made more noise than the home support and cheered us off although we lost.

We could not have got a tougher start to the season against Aberdeen, Rangers, Hearts and Celtic. The fact that we got our one point from Rangers should come as no surprise as Graeme Souness admits he doesn't like coming to Easter Road. When he does he always brings his heavy mob. I don't know why we tend to do well against Rangers. The players don't treat them any differently. Then again Celtic tend to be our bogey team, which is something else I can't explain.

Without a doubt, though, the game everyone was waiting for was the first derby of the season. The whole of Scotland had their eyes on Easter Road that day. The tension in the week before the game was the most intense since I had come to Hibs.

Of course, Wallace Mercer got himself centre stage again with media speculation on whether he would attend or not. In the end he didn't make it, but that didn't help matters one way or the other. The fans obviously felt a lot more emotional about it all than the players. Both teams that day felt a responsibility to keep cool and make sure nothing stupid happened. There was no animosity between the players. Generally there never is, although a couple on each side won't talk to the other lot, which is something I find quite stupid.

When the game actually started I thought it was a lot slower than other Hibs v Hearts games I'd played in. Usually everyone is going hell for leather from the whistle. But I did have a feeling something might happen and, sure enough, it did when John Robertson scored. He hit a speculative ball from the left and Pat McGinlay deflected it into the roof of the net. I turned round after the goal and caught sight of a guy out of the corner of my eye. It was a Hibs supporter making a beeline for wee Robbo and he grabbed him by the neck. I didn't stop to think and moved over to get the guy off the pitch. The last thing you want is a fan hitting a player or vice versa. Something like that could set everybody off. As I got hold of the Hibs fan a Hearts fan had sprinted on and took a crack at the Hibs supporter. I immediately turned on him to sort him out. The only thing on my mind was to defuse the situation and get them off the pitch. By the time the police arrived four players had apprehended the two fans.

I think the referee may have made the wrong decision when he took us off the pitch. The game could have started again and the play would have distracted the crowd. Instead tension continued to build up and it spilled over again at half-time. The whole affair was sickening, especially as the root of it was something that had nothing to do with football. When we were inside, the police asked us to walk back onto the pitch together to help calm the situation.

I'd like to stress there was absolutely no animosity among the players in the tunnel and we all felt bad for Robbo. When we got back out the game seemed to be secondary after what had happened. I was also sickened by our performance but didn't think we played as badly as people made out. I didn't have a save to make that day, whereas Henry Smith had two or three. Hearts got one own goal. We gave Craig Levein a free header for the second and Robbo was nicely positioned to obstruct my view, and their third was a good goal.

However, the game acted as a watershed and I don't think that such scenes will be repeated. Wallace Mercer took some blame afterwards on television for what happened. He had to take some responsibility. I repeat, what happened was not to do with football but actions that had taken place off the pitch. If it had happened as a result of an incident on the pitch, then the players should have taken the blame. This was not the case, but it left a sour taste that should not be associated with football.

Everything that day was a real blow for Hibs, but the young players will learn from it and how to deal with such pressure. Hopefully we can now get back to normal derbies again.

We had hit an all-time low and a lot of people had written us off. But it shows how shortsighted people can be. As our form has picked up, the chance of a place in Europe cannot be ruled out. Still some people will predict relegation one week and then a week later they will be dreaming of Europe. The Premier League is as tough as ever this season. There are no mugs, as St Johnstone have proved. Everyone will be a bit afraid of them. Rangers still have the strongest pool and it will be interesting to see if Dundee United can sustain their early challenge. Aberdeen have had another cruel blow like last season when they lost Theo Snelders. Celtic have shown a lot of style, but whether their defence is good enough is another matter. Rangers have won the league twice recently by conceding the fewest goals, and when Celtic last won it in 1988 they conceded fewest.

The lesson there is obvious. Shut the back door first if you want to win the league. However, Celtic have very exciting potential in midfield with the Paul McStay/John Collins combination. To be honest, I didn't think it would work as they're too similar but they seem to have proved me wrong. I'm confident, though, that Hibs have turned a corner and that what I came to Hibs for — European football and trophies — is within our grasp.

The turn around at the club has been remarkable when you consider how low we had sunk in the summer. Tom Farmer is already making a big contribution to the club. He didn't promise the moon, but has come up with more than the goods so far. But for him, Murdo McLeod would not be at the club. Alister Dow is sorting out the plc and Jim Gray is already proving his critics wrong.

He has taken a lot of flak from the fans, press and the share-holders. I myself have questioned him and a lot that was going on at the club. At the end of the day he has signed me up for a further three years and brought Murdo McLeod to the club. Still he can't get any praise for it. It makes you wonder what he has to do. People who cannot see the positive changes are blinkered. But I'm sure there will come a time when he gets his applause.

Meanwhile David Duff is still around on match day and is as bubbly as ever with his daft suits and jackets. He is as Hibs crazy as ever, but now has a lower profile at the club. As Hibs are making their way back on merit, I have at last made the Scotland place my own on merit.

After the World Cup I wasn't taking anything for granted, but was delighted to be first choice for our European tie against Romania. It was the first time I was in through merit rather than substituting for Jim Leighton. All I ever wanted was a chance from scratch and then it was up to me to hold onto the spot. A lot of the press said I would be playing, but they had said the same thing in Italy. So I wasn't building myself up. I had had my disappointments but there was no point in getting impatient now, after waiting for five years.

I wasn't at all nervous. I feel better every game I play for Scotland. I feel I don't have to prove myself as I did when I first arrived from Oldham. Most people are now familiar with my form in the Premier League.

Jim Leighton helped me out 100 per cent and I think he will be back. He has got an incentive to prove people wrong and he prides himself on his determination. Meanwhile I have no complacency about the number one spot.

The build-up to the Romania game was ideal for a Scotland team. Not a lot was expected after Italy so we could go out there and prove a few people wrong. Although we were hit by injuries, this only added that extra edge. Also the way the match went turned out well for us. Losing an early goal did us a favour as they sat back a bit and this made us go and look for the game.

I was delighted to see John Robertson score although it cost me a meal. I told him I would treat him if he got one and we would call it quits if I kept a clean sheet. You don't know what a risk I was taking as he's a greedy wee blighter. He cost me two bottles of champagne against Switzerland as we had the same deal again. He's a great guy and I felt he deserved his Scotland place. It took a long time coming, but having got the chance he has snapped at it.

Not long ago some Hibs fans pulled me up and said I was out of order for laughing and joking with Hearts players such as Robbo. The day I have to do that I'll pack the game in. I'd be as well playing cricket if I cannot enjoy myself in football. The point I made to them was that the majority of Hibs and Hearts fans get on really well, so why can't the players?

The Scotland squad were on a high after the Romania victory. It was a typical battling performance. Despite players dropping out of the squad since Italy, such as Maurice Johnston and Jim Bett, morale is as high as ever. The players are hungry to play for Scotland.

I don't think we have missed Maurice so far. What he did in the qualifiers for the World Cup was brilliant, but he has made his decision not to play for Scotland, so that is it. Who knows if he will regret it? He made his decision for his own reasons. You never know: he might fancy coming back if we qualify, but that would be up to Andy Roxburgh.

I wasn't too surprised at Maurice's decision. You expect the unexpected from him, but I was surprised when Jim Bett did it. I thought he had a lot he could still do for Scotland and he might want to prove something after a disappointing World Cup. I cannot understand why players make these decisions, but when all is said and done it's up to them. Against Switzerland we got a pre-match boost when we heard Bulgaria had beaten Romania 3-0, which made the game a four-pointer. Whoever won would be cruising out front. We didn't play particularly well, but got the result. Losing Paul McStay was a blow as he is someone we really need in midfield. But Steve Nicol's recall was a surprise. Jim Leighton dislocated his finger and Steve was called in and ended up rooming with me. I knew he had arrived when I came in and saw a dozen packets of crisps lying by his bed. Welcome back, Stevie! That's his hobby — scoffing crisps all day!

He seemed delighted to be back in after the breakdown in communication between Liverpool and Scotland. This again is a difficult situation. It's up to the player what he does when this arises. Does he feel strongly enough about it to defy his manager or club?

I don't suppose Hibs would ever think twice about stopping me from going as they know I would go anyway. I know they are in a different situation from Liverpool who have so many internationalists and are competing more for top honours. However, a club like Hibs haven't lost that feeling of being honoured to have their players called up. With the really big clubs their own interests seem to come before anything else.

I also thought the Swiss game was another good omen for Hibs as it was the first time for a long time that Hibs had two players in the international side — Murdo and me. The last time was in 1976 when John Blackley and Des Bremner played against Switzerland as well. Not a lot of people know that! It's a good one for Hibbies to try out on their mates in the pub. The time before was when Pat Stanton and Eric Schaedler turned out together against West Germany in 1974. Before the Argentina game Johnnie Collins and I had the chance of playing together, but nobody could tell us who were the last two Hibs players to represent Scotland in the same game. Well, now you know!

This time, though, everything went smoothly, which may be another indication of how Hibs' luck is on the upswing again. Also the night before the full international, Billy Findlay scored two goals for the Under-21s, which underlines the potential we have at Easter Road.

Both Hibs' and my own fortunes have picked up in the last few months, and here's hoping it continues. I have committed myself to the club and want to settle down in Edinburgh. I have gained a lot from coming here, but I also gave up a lot. For me still the most important thing, much more important than Hibs or Scotland, is my son Daniel.

Index